Transformation

From Broken to Blessed

Naleighna Kai

The Macro Group, LLC
Chicago, Illinois

Transformation: From Broken to Blessed
Copyright © 2021 by The Macro Group, LLC All rights reserved.

Edited by Janice M. Allen and J. L. Campbell:
jlcampbellwrites@gmail.com
Cover Designed by J. L Woodson: www.woodsoncreativestudio.com
Interior Designed by Lissa Woodson: www.naleighnakai.com
Beta Readers: D. J. Mitchell and Kelsie Maxwell

ISBN 9781952871153
ISBN 9781952871160 (E-Book)

The Macro Group, LLC
1507 E. 53rd Street, #858
Chicago, IL 60615

Scripture quotations are taken from the King James Version (KJV), public domain.

Transformation

From Broken to Blessed

Naleighna Kai

DEDICATION

Jean Woodson,
Eric Harold Spears,
LaKecia Janise Woodson,
Mildred E. Williams,
Anthony Johnson,
L. A. Banks,
Octavia Butler,
Tanishia Pearson Jones,
Emmanuel McDavid, and
Priscilla Jackson

J. L. Woodson & Donisha
Shawn Williams, Sesvalah, Ehryck, Janice
La Ammitai, Jamyi Joi, Janine Ingram, and the
members of NK's Tribe Called Success

ACKNOWLEDGEMENTS

Special thanks goes out to: The Creator from whom all Blessings and opportunities flow, Sandy (my true mother), my son, J. L. Woodson (for the awesome cover designs for this Merry Hearts series), Sesvalah, Bettye Odom, Janice M. Allen, Debra J. Mitchell, Royce Slade Morton, Bunny Ervin, J. L. Campbell, Kelly Peterson, Janine A. Ingram, Ehryck F. Gilmore, Betty Clawson, Jamyi Joy, Stephanie M. Freeman, Unique Hiram, Marie L. McKenzie, Shawn Williams, Dr. Vanessa Howard, the Kings of the Castle Ambassadors, Members of Naleighna Kai's Literary Cafe, the members of NK's Tribe Called Success, the members of Namakir Tribe, and to you, my dear readers . . . thank you all for your support.

Much love, peace, and joy,
Naleighna Kai

Naleighna Kai

There was a lasting darkness around her. Every step she took was clothed in bitterness and pain. There were no happy endings, no songs to be sung or remembered. For every tear she cried there were millions that were muted. Restoration was a myth. Healing was just as elusive.

With ten fingers and ten toes and a smile to rival the stars, darkness fled. Hope rang clear and true in his laughter. Watching him thrive and grow inspired her to do the same. Although the path seemed long and treacherous, with his hand in hers the journey was sweet. Every step decorated her soul, and every pause gave her purpose.

And just when she thought it couldn't get any better, love became flesh. With two strong arms to hold her and a muse set fire to her imagination her journey was just beginning.

—Stephanie M. Freeman, *author of Necessary Evil, Unfinished Business,* and *Nature of the Beast*

Chapter 1

The Passion

Amnon sprawled on the cushion, closed his eyes, and groaned. "I want Tamar. I can't get her out of my mind."

His cousin, Jonadab, settled in the space beside him, clasping his shoulder with one hand. "Aren't you a king's son? Why should you want for anything? Tall, dark, handsome, and filthy rich … means the world is yours."

"The world maybe, but not her," Amnon said, shrugging off a hand that had turned an even darker shade from spending too much time in the sun chasing the more available women of the kingdom. The two most eligible bachelors were constantly mistaken for one another because they so closely resembled in physical appearance—dark brown eyes, lips ready to break out in a smirk at any moment, rugged features that made them easy on the eyes—at least that's what everyone said. And they milked that goat for every single drop.

At the moment, he was irritated that his cousin was making all the points he'd already made to himself.

"You could marry her," Jonadab suggested with a lift of his eyebrows.

"First, she's a virgin." After a deep breath, he added, "She's too closely related according to Hebrew law, and I'm not ready to get married to her, or anyone."

Jonadab was silent for a few moments, then said, "Maybe you could take her as a concubine."

"She's King David's daughter, man. Definitely not concubine material." Amnon massaged his temples as if they were a genie's lamp from which a puff of smoke would emerge, followed by someone who could magically change his unfortunate circumstance.

"And to be honest, her brother Absalom is a little on the crazy side. I don't want none of that smoke."

Jonadab crossed one leg over the other. "So what are you going to do?"

"What can I do?" Amnon yelled, glaring at his cousin. "It is what it is."

Two servants made their way past them to the royal chambers. Both of them gave Amnon a wide smile and held out an offering of fruit and figs. He waved them away, but Jonadab lifted a few for himself and received the "evil eye" from the taller of the two women.

"See, everyone loves you," Jonadab said, feeling a little disappointed that they didn't give him the same consideration. "Especially your father. He'll give you anything you desire, even Tamar. You just have to ask for the right thing."

Amnon narrowed his gaze on the man who wasn't merely his cousin, but also his best friend in all of Israel. "You're talking fast and believe I'm thinking slow. You heard what I said, and you're *still* not making any kind of sense."

Jonadab released a weary sigh. "You know, the more I teach you, the dumber—"

"Don't even say it," Amnon snapped, before he could finish with "the dumber you get."

"Well, someone needs to. You're the one with the hots for your sister."

"Half-sister," Amnon countered.

"Semantics," he shot back.

"She's still blood," Amnon quipped, snagging one of the figs before Jonadab could put it into his mouth. "And still off-limits. She's a virgin."

Jonadab quirked an eyebrow. "Not if you have a plan."

While growing up, there had never been a time when Jonadab and Amnon weren't getting into some kind of trouble. Jonadab had been the planner on most occasions, while Amnon provided the money and muscle. Didn't matter to their mothers, though. Trouble was trouble, no matter how one sliced it. But Tamar was the type of trouble they should never get into, even if she was one of the most beautiful maidens in the kingdom.

She lived in the women's quarters, far away from where Amnon and Jonadab resided. Tamar couldn't make a move unless one of those blasted eunuchs was with her. The mission his cousin was trying to pull off was next to impossible. On the plus side, Jonadab had never steered him too far wrong—maybe into wrong, but that was beside the point.

"I'm listening."

Jonadab gave a low, throaty chuckle. "Slow or fast?"

Amnon glared, causing Jonadab to cut off his laughter and raise his hand in mock surrender. "See, what you should do is play like you're not feeling well and—"

"What does that get me?"

"A day in bed."

Amnon waved him off. "Oh, like that solves the problem."

"Alone."

He gave his friend a serious side-eye. "Oh, that *really* solves the problem."

An evil glint lit Jonadab's eyes. "With no one to hear her cries for help."

The understanding of the plan clicked at that very moment. "Oh."

"Right." Jonadab's lips lifted in a smirk. "Now who's listening slow?"

Amnon shook the crumbs from his robe, grumbling, "Why do you insist on bringing up old things?"

"Because it seems I need to spell out everything as if you ..." He shook his head. "Anyway, pretend that you're sick and ask your father to have Tamar tend to your needs."

"Seriously?"

"No, I don't mean *those* kinds of needs," he clarified, frowning. "I mean to feed you and all that. Food, actual food. He doesn't have to know that you're going to have her feed *another* type of need."

The two of them remained silent, each stewing in their own thoughts as the nightly breeze wafted into the palace, shifting their tunics about their sandals.

Amnon asked, "Do you think that will work?"

"I guarantee it," Jonadab replied. "You are his favorite, and heir to the throne. Besides, who is he to deny you anything you want after what he did with Bathsheba."

Amnon grinned, seeing the possibility of this plan working in his favor for that reason alone. "Well, there is that."

Chapter 2

THE PLAN

"What on earth is wrong with you?" David asked, rushing into Amnon's chambers with several servants on his heels. "All the servants are acting like you're about to cross over into eternity."

The health of a man who would be king was serious business. The royal physicians had come and gone but couldn't find anything wrong with Amnon, who was playing the role of a man on the brink of death to the hilt.

"Father, I'm really not feeling so good," he groaned.

David peered at him for several moments, his lips pursed in disapproval as though seriously weighing things. Standing to his full height, he said, "All right, I'll have more servants come in. They'll take good care of you."

Jonadab sent Amnon a warning look by widening his eyes to the size of saucers.

"Father, I don't want anyone to see me like this," Amnon protested, gripping the edges of the cloths covering his body. "Only family. Maybe one of my sisters."

David grimaced and narrowed his gaze, totally missing Jonadab's vigorous shake of the head. "Servants have seen your naked tailbone since you could fill out a loincloth."

"He does have a point," Jonadab mumbled.

Amnon grimaced as he asked, "Whose side are you on?"

"Mine."

"Figures," David and Amnon said in unison.

"Servants talk, Father," Amnon continued in a raspy voice. "Remember what happened with you and—"

"You do have a point," David chimed in before his son could add the name Bathsheba, another family drama that was a source of pain.

Acting as if he only had a minute left to live, Amnon perched on the edge of the bed, wiping his brow.

Jonadab inched out of David's peripheral vision, signaling with a twirl of his fingers that Amnon should move things along. Then he quickly reclaimed the space he'd vacated.

"Maybe I'll eat something, if my sister prepares it for me," Amnon offered, straining to raise his hands. "I'm too weak to lift anything."

"But not too weak to move your mouth and make requests." David rubbed his long beard, that could have used a serious trim, at the same moment that Amnon rolled his eyes. "Who do you want me—"

"Tamar."

Jonadab slid a hand across his neck, signaling his friend into silence.

Meanwhile, Amnon almost kicked himself for being too obvious.

"No." The king's voice was firm. "I'll send one of the servant's daughters."

"No, it has to be Tamar."

Both David and Jonadab snapped their attention Amnon's way, causing him to add, "I mean, she's not doing much of anything right now. And I heard she's a better cook than some of the others. Didn't they almost kill the royal advisor at the last feast because the meat was undercooked?"

"Tamar?" David ventured, still studying him as though trying to understand the logic behind the request.

"She's so devout and discreet," he said, placing a trembling hand on his forehead. "We need that right about now. This family can't stand yet *another* scandal."

David pondered that for several moments, then in a resigned tone he said, "I'll send her right away."

Out of David's line of sight, Jonadab did a victory fist pump as Amnon ground out, "Thank you. Thank you so much."

David made his way to the exit but turned back to face them. "I really think you two should stop hanging together. You're always up to no good." He waggled a finger at Jonadab. "Especially you."

Jonadab pulled an imaginary dagger out of his heart. "King David, you wound me."

"And he's a comedian, too," David said in a dry tone, then walked a few feet and paused. "I don't know. Something is not right."

"But you're still sending Tamar, right?"

Jonadab gave Amnon a hard look that shut him up.

"Sure. Whatever. Why do I get the feeling that this is going to come back and bite me on the hindquarters?" David's tone lowered to a mutter as he stared at them for another long moment. "And if he's supposed to be so ill, why are you sticking around?" He gestured for one of the servants to usher Jonadab out of the room.

Chapter 3

The Process

Then David sent word to Tamar, saying, "Go to your brother Amnon's house, and feed him."

She left her quarters and entered the throne room.

"Feed him?" she asked, staring at her father as her own servants gave him a quizzical look. "Doesn't he ... doesn't he have his own servants for that?"

David paused as though considering something she couldn't understand. "He wants you to do it."

* * *

Tamar shuddered and pulled the multi-colored robe around her form, trying to make sense of what had transpired. How had such a simple act of kindness, a command from her father, gone so horribly wrong?

Amnon had sent all of the servants away. Every single one. Now she knew why. He waited until she was tired from making those cakes, knowing that kneading dough was rigorous work. The man wasn't ill at all. He was slick, sly, and wicked.

"So, you wanted me—specifically—to bring you a meal and this is what you had in mind?" she screamed. "To dishonor me this way? My father will have something to say about this."

Amnon raised up, resting his cheek on the palm of a hand, and gave her a half smile but only hatred existed in his eyes. "Who's going to believe you? You're a woman. And no one heard you cry for help. There were no witnesses."

She lifted her chin, trying to hold on to a little bit of hope when she said, "I am King David's daughter."

"And I'm his son," he shot back. "Next in line to be king. Who will they believe?"

Tamar leaned against the wall, trying to make sure she didn't slide to the floor since her legs threatened to give out. She also ached, but would tend to her injuries when she finished dealing with this scoundrel. "You could've asked our father for my hand in marriage rather than do this horrible thing."

"Marriage wasn't even a consideration," he taunted, dismissing her with a wave. "And it's done now. You can leave."

Fear stabbed her heart.

"So that's what you're doing right now?" she said, trying to hold the angst and despair at bay. "You commit a heinous act and don't have the decency to make things right? Now you want to send me away? What kind of ..." She shook her head, then lowered her gaze to the floor. "Sending me away like nothing happened; that's worse than what you've already done."

"Tough. Get your things and leave. I can't stand the sight of you." He slid the platter so far off the bed that the freshly-baked cakes splattered across the floor. "And take this horrible tasting food, too."

She glanced at the mess he'd made, and then to her thighs, which showed evidence of the earlier, more horrific one he had made that now stained her garment of diverse colors, the one that only the king's virgin daughters were supposed to wear. "I'm not leaving until you make this right."

"Oh?" He tilted his head, narrowed an angry gaze and yelled, "Servants."

Several of them came running.

"Take her. Now!" He gestured toward Tamar in the most dismissive flourish she'd ever witnessed from him or any man. "Put this woman out of my sight."

The three of them swept a look first to Tamar, then to Amnon, and gave each other a frightened glance before the oldest of them complied and rushed to do his bidding.

"Don't do this," she pleaded to Amnon as the servants paused in their movements. "Please don't destroy my life this way."

They looked to him for direction, wanting to see if her pleas fell on compassionate ears.

"Did you hear me?" he said through his teeth with a glower at the servants.

"You know they already have my marriage arranged," she protested while the servants gently guided her toward the doorway. "That's not something that can happen now."

"Sounds like king's daughter problems to me."

The servants took hold of her trembling body, dragging her from the room as she cried, "This is going to taint both of us. I can never marry. I can never have children. I'll be an outcast among our people."

"Once again, sounds like *your* problem," he said, shooing her from the room and ignoring the sorrowful look one of the servants gave him. "It's definitely not my problem."

The servants brought her out and shut the door.

On the way back to her quarters, Tamar tore her garment to strips. After sprinkling ashes on her head, she released continuous wails that told of her pain.

Chapter 4

The Aftermath

"He did what?" Absalom roared loud enough to shake the palace walls.

The women relayed the story that Tamar had told them.

"Are they telling the truth? He did this to you?"

"Yes."

Absalom stared at the women lined up before him, his expression went from anger, to confusion, and ended with a thunderous frown. Several minutes later, his gaze locked on Tamar as he said, "Don't say anything to anyone."

"But he—"

"Do not tell anyone what he did," he warned. "Hold your peace."

Absalom sank into the nearest chair and thought things over for several minutes. No one moved as they watched him come up with the next steps.

"Pack your things. You're coming to stay with me."

Tamar's sigh of pain was audible as she wiped her tears. "Thank you, my brother. Thank you."

* * *

"What are you going to do about it?" Absalom's deafening voice echoed all the way to the servant's quarters. "You need to marry her according to custom to restore what little honor she has left."

"Well that's not going to happen," Amnon said in a sarcastic tone that made Absalom's blood boil.

"What are you going to do?" Absalom asked, shifting his body so he angled toward their father. "Tell the king who you've arranged Tamar's marriage with that someone borrowed her virginity with no intention of giving it back?"

"Marriage between brother and sister is prohibited," David said. "Punishable by death."

"I don't consider him a brother," Absalom snapped. "Name him what he is … a rapist."

"Stop calling me that."

"I call it like I see it," Absalom shot back, circling around his half-brother, fists clenched by his side. "You need to make this right."

"I'm not marrying her."

"Do something," Absalom said in a defiant tone to their father, who shrugged and asked, "What do you propose? I can't force him to marry her."

Absalom adjusted his tunic and squared his shoulders. "But he forced her to do something she didn't want to do. So, what's the difference?"

"It is what it is," Amnon said around a bite of an apple. "I'm not marrying her."

Absalom shifted a gaze to David once again. "And you're really not going to do anything?"

"What can I do?"

He shook his fist at his father. "You could protect your daughter the same way you're protecting your worthless son."

"The matter is out of my hands," David replied, pulling his robe about his body and standing at his full height that was still a few inches less than his son.

After a moment, Absalom smiled, but it was a bitter gesture. "That's fine."

Not sure if it was the tone of Absalom's voice or maybe his stance, David warned, "Don't do anything reckless."

"Right."

"'Vengeance is mine,' saith the Lord."

Absalom shrugged and replied, "You know, I'm more of an eye for an eye kind of guy."

"You're thinking about taking more than an eye," David roared, understanding full well what his son's words meant, and the actions that would follow. "You aim to take his life."

"He took her life."

"That's not the same."

"It is ... to her." Absalom shook a finger in his father's direction. "She trusted you to keep her safe. Even you're smart enough to realize he had planned this all along. He specifically requested that she come. You didn't think it strange that he wanted to be alone with her in his private chambers? And he did it under the guise of being ill." He raked a gaze over Amnon from head to toe. "If he was so sick, that was the most miraculous recovery I've ever witnessed. He did it deliberately, and you're letting him get away with it. Just like you nearly got away with what *you* did."

Absalom stabbed a finger in David's chest. "But God was watching then, and He's watching now. Your son is no different than you. You saw Bathsheba and conspired to have her. Could Bathsheba really refuse the King? You wanted. He wanted. You had her. He raped her. Like father. Like son."

David shifted his gaze first to Amnon, whose smirk was not making things any better. Then he looked at Absalom and warned, "If you take his life, you're going to pay for that."

"You're going to make *me* pay," he countered. "But you didn't make *him* pay because a son is worth far more than a daughter, right?"

"Who am I to pass judgment?" David protested, now pacing in front of the throne. "Like you just pointed out, I have sins of my own."

Absalom turned his back on his father, looking out over the palace grounds. "But that doesn't make what was done to Tamar right in any shape, form, or fashion."

"What can I do? The damage is already done."

"You could've been a father instead of a king. She needed her father. Since that didn't happen, her brother might have to step in."

Chapter 5

THE BIG PAYBACK

And it came to pass after two full years, that Absalom had sheepshearers in Baalhazor, which is beside Ephraim: and Absalom invited all the king's sons.

Then Absalom had an audience with the king, saying, "We have some sheepshearers nearby. You should let my brother Amnon go with us."

David peered up at him from his throne. "Why should he go anywhere with you?"

"Because it will be a big event." Absalom pleaded with him several times for Amnon and all the king's sons to go.

King David nodded with reluctance. "Somehow, I really don't get a good feeling about this."

* * *

Absalom stood outside of the gathering while everyone was eating and making merry. He pulled his servants to the side. "The minute Amnon's all up in liquor, hit him and kill him."

The servants glanced uncomfortably at each other.

"Don't be afraid. I'm giving the orders here," he said, realizing they were still worried. "I should have done something sooner. Someone needed to look out for my sister. My father was too knee-deep in his own stuff to handle the business, so I need to take care of it for him."

"If you do this," one of the servants warned. "You'll lose any rights to the throne."

"My sister is worth it. Amnon does not deserve to be breathing, and I certainly don't believe my father should put him on the throne." He took a few steps to the door and peered inside the room at his brother, who was on his fourth goblet of wine. "My father allowed my sister to be humiliated before the entire court. I think I should return the favor."

Shaking his head, Absalom's servant said, "That's a dangerous game."

"These are dangerous times."

And the servants of Absalom did unto Amnon as Absalom had commanded. Then all the king's sons arose, and every man gat him up upon his mule, and fled.

* * *

David woke from a deep sleep. The sense of foreboding that had been on his heart all night long was worse than ever.

A servant rushed inside, saying, "Absalom killed all of your sons. There isn't a single one of them left breathing."

Upon hearing that news, King David ripped the garments from his body and stretched out on the ground, consumed with grief. The servants tore their clothes to shreds as well.

Jonadab walked in and asked what was going on. When a servant shared the story, he corrected them by saying, "No, that's not what happened. They didn't take out all of your sons. Only Amnon is dead. Absalom's been plotting this since the day Amnon forced his sister."

foundation tried to understand why it was going on. When a
servant showed the smile he corrected them by saying, "No,
that's not what happened." They didn't... but not after this...
technically Amon is dead. Abiodun... been plotting this since
the day Amon threw his sister...

Chapter 6

BLESSING IN DISGUISE

Like Tamar, who wasn't protected and loved by her father, I, too had an experience where mine didn't protect me. He didn't respect my right to say no. My uncle didn't respect my right to say no. That's on top of the fact that I was adopted by my biological mother, and the physical and mental abuse was nothing short of exponential. So by the time I was fourteen, my body and soul were damaged to the point that I needed to heal. Family had done a number on me, so the relationships I attracted from that point on were a direct reflection of what I had been reduced to—a mere shadow of what I was intended to be.

My first experience with unconditional love was a tiny, unexpected bundle of joy.

All right, I'm going to be honest. Considering what I had been through early in life, I didn't think there was a maternal bone in my body. So what happened to me at age eighteen? Right at the point when I was about to put a "for sale" sign on one thigh and an "open for business" sign on the other? You guessed it, that star in the east floated by, along with Three Wise Men. In either case, I was now expecting the one thing I didn't believe I could handle. How was I going to raise a child—a *man* child—without infecting him with the aftermath of my traumatic experiences? Why would The Creator put me in such a predicament? Were they passing the peace pipe up there in Heaven?

On the whole, I felt taking care of the basics would be easy: breastfeeding, diapers, shelter, and all that. What worried me was the emotional aspects of his upbringing. Mentally and spiritually, was I equipped to navigate him safely to maturity? Especially since his father—a male who was eight years older than my seventeen years when we dated—had decided that being a father was not part of his plans. He abandoned both of us to become a perpetual student in order to avoid paying child support. I should've guessed something was a little off about him when he asked me out on a date while my head was half-covered in hair relaxer. But I digress.

My son arrived, and he was absolutely beautiful. Actually, I'm exaggerating, because he looked like he'd been through the wringer. He had ivory skin, purple lips, and slanted eyes, which made me swear up and down they were passing off the wrong child to me. Maybe they needed to place him back in the oven and put him on broil for a few minutes. Thankfully, he soon fleshed out and became a beautiful little bundle of joy. And that's truth.

Motherhood was especially rewarding. Here was someone who depended on me for everything. A little person who seemed to live for my smiles, my hugs, my voice. A person who needed my protection. A person who I would keep safe at all costs. A person who would inspire me to take risks I would not have dared on my own. Even buying my first house at nineteen years old was due to the determination to have a safe place to raise my son. The neighbors I stayed with from time to time because my mother and I weren't getting along, were losing their home. When they moved out of the property to allow the foreclosure process to move forward, I slid in and changed the utilities into my name.

At the time, my only source of income was public assistance, definitely not enough to truly live on, but it kept us afloat until the Veteran's Administration came calling. They owned the property and found that I was maintaining the premises. Fortunately, they gave me the opportunity to purchase the home. I landed a position with the City of Chicago, and combined with Avon sales and the fact that I had a crew of high school students selling chocolate fundraiser candy bars to help me come up with the down payment, I was able to qualify for the house. The man who worked for the V.A. gave me grace, and The Creator showed me favor.

All I knew was that I wanted a house, and this one was three doors down from my mother. The perfect starter home—three bedrooms, one bath, kitchen, living room, and basement. Trust me, I didn't know anything about the regular progression of life—apartment, *then* a house. I wasn't taught any of that. Nothing about saving, building credit, or anything.

My original limiting belief was that my life was supposed to be lived in pain. My original limiting belief was that I was supposed to experience lack and limitation. My original limiting belief was that I could only live paycheck to paycheck. My original limiting belief was that I had to struggle to make ends meet, before I met the end.

My mother wasn't taught to balance a checkbook, so she couldn't teach me. Therefore, I didn't teach my son. Which meant the cycle would continue if someone didn't embrace a different way of living. That someone had to be me.

Then I learned about the law of attraction and even the mere possibility of being prosperous. There's a Bible verse that says, *The blessing of the LORD, it maketh rich, and he addeth no sorrow with it.* Proverbs 10:22

Armed with that knowledge, my thinking shifted. What I did was attract an understanding that struggle was not my birthright. What I did was attract the resources, books, and people who could teach me a better way. What I also did was attract the things I desired, which made me flex my faith muscle, which also came with an understanding that I had to put in the work. I could have faith all day long, but if it wasn't followed by intentions and actions, it would be nothing more than wishful thinking. Only by shaking off that original birthright and pattern was I able to expand my consciousness and accept that I *could* be wealthy, which eventually transformed into I *should* be wealthy.

Build that prosperity muscle by doing something as simple as expressing your gratefulness for being able to have your bills on autopay.

You're grateful that your bills are covered at little or no cost to you.

You're grateful that what you need is already there before you even ask.

Start claiming it and let that faith muscle become stronger, then ask for that $1,000, that $10,000 more, that $100,000 more, then that million, and even more.

Create a vision board and write out a check for each one of your bills—mortgage, car note, student loan, and script Paid in Full across each one.

It is your birthright to prosper, but you also have to open your mind, heart, and soul to that possibility by putting in the mental, spiritual, physical, and financial work.

You were not put on this earth to struggle. You were put here to be victorious. And it starts with embracing that you could be—no, actually you should be, prosperous.

I am come that they might have life, and that they might have it more abundantly. John 10:10

When my son was six months old, I hadn't been taught any of these principles of abundance. I was still reeling from the blows life had whopped upside my head and other places. What I had was such a strong desire to have my own home that it manifested in a miraculous way. And it came from *acting as if* I already had the space. When I was still living in my mother's home, I purchased new dishes, bed linen, silverware, and glasses, and hid them under my son's crib. To this day, when I'm ready to move into a new space, those are the first items I purchase. It's my way of saying, "All right, Creator, I'm handling my business while you're handling everything else." The books: *Act As If: Think It Into Existence* by Ehryck F. Gilmore, CH and *Speak it into Existence* by Rev. Renee Sesvalah Cobb-Dishman are wonderful to read to help with this process.

So, I now had my own home three doors down from my mother and could raise my son my way. My mother was so angered that I wouldn't let her take over raising my son that she treated him differently. Her actions were obvious to everyone. Only later did my son pick up on her attitude, and he was saddened by it. He loved his grandmother. Truly loved her. But she only saw him as an extension of me. She hated the fact that I desired for my son to turn out better than my brother and nephews.

My mother was partial to boys and spoiled them rotten. That was not how I wanted my son to grow up. Even at nineteen, I felt that the best thing I could do as a parent was make sure he was a good person, able to take care of himself, live out his life's desires, and achieve more than I ever had. Never wanted him to experience any of the sexual abuse that I had, nor did I want him to be spoiled, lazy, and unable to take responsibility for his actions or his life.

My son had such a wonderful disposition that people wanted to give him everything, because he asked for nothing. That smile, that voice, that face—that sweetness in his soul that did not reflect me or his father. He was never materialistic and that made people do more for him than he realized. For his birthday, he wanted to have friends and family over—it was never about presents.

He also did not like to disappoint people. All I had to do was point out something that wasn't right, and he was instantly sorry for what he'd done wrong.

But sometimes I took it a step further. A step too far. At one point, I ended up having him stay with his Godmother for a while because he almost burned the house down with a gift of fireworks from his father that he hid in the hamper near the heating element in his bedroom! My son was so afraid of the punishment I might dole out that he ran out of the house, butt naked, in the dead of winter, with six feet of snow on the ground.

Years later, when he was going off to his freshman year at Fisk University, I apologized to him. He deserved to be disciplined—a rare occurrence of about once a year—but not with a severity that put such a primal fear in him. He did not deserve that. As a mother, and one who has grown spiritually, I recognized that and was so grateful for his forgiveness. He did write about his experience in the book, *Superwoman's Child: Son of a Single Mother*. Recounting the incident from his point of view didn't necessarily put me in the best light. He asked my permission before putting it in print. I told him that it was his story, his truth, and I would not censure him in any way. Writing was his way of healing, and parents reading it would definitely understand.

The Creator knew to pair me up with the perfect child to facilitate a series of lessons of loving someone outside of myself. My relationship with my son also opened me to realizing there were more important things in life than the darkness I'd experienced growing up. And on another note, the same holds true for my son. He needed to come through a particular set of parents because he had his own series of lessons to learn and challenges to overcome.

Sometimes the thing we think we don't want is the very thing we need for our spiritual development. We'll swear up and down that we'll never do X, Y, or Z. And The Creator says, "Oh, yeah? Let Me see what we can do about that." Basically, it's because energy follows thought. When you put emphasis on what you *don't* want, it's taking the focus off the things you *do* want. And trust me, the things you don't want always come with a calling card—*remember that statement you made a kabillion years ago? Well, since you feel so strongly about it, you must really want to tackle it.* And then … BAM! Suddenly you're paddling upstream without a boat or a paddle. You're now grappling with a challenge that you swore you never wanted to wade through in the first place.

There were more important things in life than the darkness I'd experienced arriving up. And on another note, we are fonder lying to myself. He needed to come through a return phase of parents because he had his own series of lessons to learn and challenges to overcome.

Sometimes the thing we think we don't want is the very thing we need for our spiritual development. Will we at no need down that we're headed X...

"..." ... whatever ... to about her. I secretly ... follow the ... When something troubled...

Chapter 7

IN DIVINE ORDER

In all honesty, my son almost didn't make it here. The first two months of my pregnancy, I was deathly ill. Couldn't keep water down. Was bringing stuff back up that didn't look anything like what I'd eaten. Three months into turning eighteen, in college, living at home, and pregnant.

My body went through a similar rocky experience a year earlier with my first pregnancy and miscarriage. The two months prior, my mother and I were in a tug-of-war. One evening, she fixed butter beans for dinner. I did not like them, Sam I am, and would not eat them with green eggs and ham. My mother was insulted and proclaimed that if I didn't eat them, I couldn't eat anything else in her house.

Well, that was fine by me. I would just eat at school. The lunchroom ladies would feed me. That is, until my mother's spies came back and told her what was happening. When my mother figured out she wasn't winning this particular battle, she then said if I didn't eat at home, I couldn't eat anywhere else.

So, for a month I was on water only and thought I was sick

because I wasn't eating. I only took a pregnancy test because my cycle had stopped.

The day I found out I was pregnant was the same day I miscarried. Earlier, I had several skirmishes with my sister, Eve, who was also pregnant. My mother and true mother had taken a trip to California at the time. Those encounters with Eve led to me staying locked in my room, while placing a few calls to the police.

One of the dispatch women asked my sister while I was listening on another extension, "Honey, where is y'all's mother?"

My sister replied, "She's in California."

The dispatch lady shot back, "If I had raised two fools, I'd be in California, too."

That night, I was in such pain, and my sister just watched as I crawled down the stairs to get help. The ambulance took me to the nearest hospital, but I lost the baby along the way. I will forever remember the kindness and compassion of those two emergency personnel.

So a year later, I was pregnant again. I did not want to be pregnant, and my body was doing all it could to accommodate my mindset. The doctors eventually decided they had to take the baby, or else both of us might die. On the night before I was scheduled for the procedure, I had a dream that changed my entire life.

In the dream, I was an Asian woman, a lower wife/concubine of an Emperor. Every other wife had given him daughters. I was the only one who gave birth to a son. They took my son then put me and my two daughters out of the palace. Every day for a year, rain or shine, I was at the gate crying, wailing for the return of my son. Finally, they brought him to me and dragged me away from the gate. I didn't care, we were so happy he was in my arms. The four of us were walking and came to a tunnel. In this tunnel, the daughters disappeared and soon the faces of people I recognized in this lifetime appeared, mostly from the Baptist Church I attended at that time. Sister Dorothy, Bessie Sims, Aridell Slaughter all came forth bringing gifts for me and my son, and told me that we would be all right.

When I woke, it was time for me to leave the house and go to the hospital. I didn't. For the first time in two months I had a full meal. And it wasn't a lightweight breakfast kind of thing either. Leftovers of Salisbury steak, mashed potatoes and gravy, mixed vegetables with lots of corn, and biscuits, and some Kool-Aid. (Yes, red—the best kind!). This stayed down, and so did every meal thereafter.

I wanted my child.

Michael Reese Hospital, where I gave birth to him, was a teaching hospital. I didn't quite understand what that meant, and was none too pleased when a crew of doctors came in and all of them started checking out "the goods." I told the doctor I was going to charge admission. He said, "But we're only hanging out in the lobby."

I replied, "Yes, but the view of the movie is still the same. Pay up."

They laughed so hard that they couldn't do anything else for a few moments before he ushered all of them out of the room.

J. L. fell asleep while I was in labor. The nurses had to come in and shake my stomach from time to time. Shoot, if he knew what I knew about what was waiting on this side of things, he'd have continued to stay inside. During those twenty-six hours of labor, I read three novels, plus eight Harlequin romances, and took notes on everything. I kept a journal from pregnancy to delivery, writing in it regularly until he was six, then turning it over to him to continue. Those journal entries became part of his first book, *The Things I Could Tell You*, written at fifteen years old and published at sixteen. A book deal for his second book, *Superwoman's Child: Son of a Single Mother*, came from Simon & Schuster soon after.

Year after year, my son never ceased to amaze me. Overall, I thought, "Hey, this motherhood thing isn't so bad after all." I enrolled in classes to adopt more children.

Then my son hit puberty and lost his entire mind on a more permanent basis.

Soon, the adoption people were calling me, saying, "You haven't been to classes lately." Frustrated as I was at the time, I promptly replied, "Sweetheart, let me tell you something. I don't want this little _____ I already have, and I don't want your little _____s either." Remember, I wasn't Little Miss Sunshine, so I'll let you fill in the blanks.

She asked my son's age. When I said twelve, she laughed and asked me to call them back in a couple of years.

They're still waiting.

Now, here's the interesting part. That period of my life was a rough time all around, and it probably had less to do with my son's antics—some of which were life-threatening, due to his father's intervention—than the fact that I had finally found the courage to tell my true mother what had happened to me during those two months I lived with my father the summer of my fourteenth year.

After my confession, as expected, she was ready to end his life.

My father was taken to the hospital two days later with blood poisoning. No, it wasn't her handiwork or mine, but that timing, though. If I had told her back when it first happened at age fourteen, she would've killed him. But I needed her more than justice needed to be served.

Being his only known living relative, I spent two months going back and forth to Olympia Fields Hospital to handle his medical care. Finally one day, a friend of mine said, "He's waiting for you to forgive him."

In my heart, forgiveness was the last thing he deserved. But I had to give it some thought. My father's condition was such that he couldn't move a muscle, nor could he take in proper food sustenance. He couldn't even blink his lids across eyes that stayed open 24/7. Almost a mirror image of some of the things I experienced under his roof. The doctor let me know they needed to remove the skin from around his genitals because it was turning blue.

I finally gave in, stood by his bedside and said, "Daddy, I forgive you."

When I made it home that day, the hospital had called and left a message. My father had passed away not long after I left his room.

Now for the reality of things. It took *years* for that statement of forgiveness to become a reality. Mostly because the real issue was that the person I truly needed to forgive was *myself*. Thoughts of "If only I had stayed and endured my biological mother's abuse", "If only I had the stomach for what my aunt was setting me up to do." "If only … then none of this would have happened."

So at the same time my son was having an out-of-body puberty experience, I was having one of my own. Well, not the puberty part, but this wasn't the best time for either of us. My reaction to what was going on with him made me look even deeper at myself, which put me on the initial path of healing.

J.L. was in his own world of pain, wondering what was so wrong with him—a karate, football, and baseball champ, an honor student—that his father didn't love him.

Me? I was wondering what was so wrong with me that The Creator would start my life by giving me a ringside seat by the fire, next to Satan himself.

Fast forward to December 1999. I finally was able to write about my experiences, weaving them into a fictional format so there was some objectivity. I never understood why I fell into writing. The "how" was pretty interesting in itself, and something I'll tell at another time.

Soon after publishing *She Touched My Soul*, I started receiving emails from women who had been through similar circumstances. One woman flew in from New Jersey to meet the real-life counselor, who was a character in my book. She also needed the type of healing that I had experienced.

This is how I found my purpose—healing. Overcoming pain, obstacles, and challenges. I didn't know a novel could help with that. Some women will probably never seek help. I didn't. My boss at the social service agency where I worked eventually became my sexual abuse counselor. After hearing a little of my story, she later became my pastor, and even more importantly, one of my best friends. She came into my life when the timing was exactly right.

Some women might not ever pick up the type of books that could point them toward counseling or something else that would help them to heal; such as *You Can Heal Your Life* or *Empowering Women* (both by Louise Hay). But some of them picked up *She Touched My Soul*, *Loving Me for Me*, *My Time in the Sun*, or *Was it Good For You Too?*—all novels penned by me—and they were helped in some way.

My writing also changed the people who were around me. And my life, my inner circle, is now filled with people who love me unconditionally.

Chapter 8

I'll Always Have Your Back

Something interesting happened at work one day. In the middle of handling the travel expenses for one of my wonderful female attorneys, things didn't quite add up. *Hmmm ... two bottles of beer and two glasses of wine at dinner in a body that is much too tiny to soak it all up in that short span of time. No, that's not like her at all.*

Some legal assistants would have let it slide and allowed the accounting people to call her on the carpet about charging so many drinks to the firm. Even though I didn't know whether she indulged or not, I knew *that* much liquor was out of character for her. Now if it had been the partner I worked for at that time, that man could drink me, you, and everyone in the building under the table—no problemo.

Before lunch, I walked into my lady lawyer's office, showed

her the tab, and asked, "Hey, is there any chance you had this dinner with someone else?"

She frowned, then her eyes grew as wide as saucers. "OMG, yes! I certainly didn't have all those drinks myself."

"I kinda thought that," I replied, giving her a smile.

She circled the items that were hers, which didn't include *any* of those four drinks. "Thank you for catching that."

To which I replied, "That's what I'm here for. I'll always have your back."

Remember those words ... I'll always have your back.

Several years ago, I met someone who was totally out of character for me. I thought The Creator knew me. But if that were true, why did a bad boy from the wrong side of the tracks drop into my life the moment I walked into my favorite Jamaican restaurant? Seriously? This was the best The Creator could do? I mean, on book deals, tours, getting my son in college, getting me into a wonderful apartment with a lake view, acquiring this job—and now He wanted to send me *who*? Awww, come on.

For two years, I had written intentions of things I wanted in my life. Everything from prosperity, to book deals, to the right job. When I finally healed, I wrote about a mate and focused on what I wanted to experience in a relationship—peace, unconditional love, compassion, respect, honor, joy, understanding, excellent communication—about thirty attributes on that sheet. I didn't write that I wanted short, sunburnt, and sensational, or tall, tan, and terrific. I simply listed the *experiences* I wanted to have with that special someone.

Two years passed and nothing happened. Not a single thing. Then I finally became angry and said to The Creator, "All right, if it's going to take a minute, then could you at least send me a placeholder until the real deal comes along?"

That line was said in anger because all other things—new car, hitting the *Essence* bestseller's list, the start of being debt-free—had already come to pass. But this whole unconditional love thing must have been a Veggie Whopper of a request— because all I heard was "crickets" in that department.

Helloooooo. Are you hearing me up there? Is there an echo in the house?

So, when I added that whole "if it's going to be a minute" line, I was angry.

And The Creator gave me back what I put out. Enough to fulfill my request and shut me up at the same time. And more than enough to prove I wasn't ready for what had been requested. The experience taught me that I needed to *get* ready because the real thing was going to meet me at a certain "level-place-consciousness". And to be honest, I certainly wasn't there yet.

Yes, The Creator has a wicked sense of humor.

I'll always have your back.

Now here's this person—a younger man—who was totally out of my element; totally out of character; totally not within my wheelhouse; who stepped to the forefront and into that space. Had me asking what the heck did I create in my life? What did I ask for?

But let me tell you, that man brought me a set of lessons that practically forced me to splinter my soul into four separate books to analyze, appreciate, and recognize what I was supposed to take away from them. I only had three months with him—a placeholder. Three whole months and the most powerful love lesson of all.

At that time, I intimidated him—a little. All right, maybe more than just a little. Mostly because, in his mind, I was up here (hands above my head). The relationship was interesting because I never knew what to expect since, in my mind, we had absolutely nothing in common.

When Tony came to my apartment, he would stand in the center of the living room, admiring the beauty of it; how clean it was; how neatly everything fit in place; how sparse it was. I'm a minimalist and don't believe in clutter or filling up every bit of space, and it showed. The quiet, the peace—sanctuary. *That* was what impressed him more than anything. Only later would I learn that I—just by being myself—was what impressed him most of all.

What set us on our spiritual journey was him opening up to me on the very first night, being vulnerable, sharing his truth—a truth that frightened me at first.

Really? You're going to test me this way? was my question to The Creator.

I'll always have your back.

Let me be honest. He worked at the place I first saw him— one of my favorite restaurants. But he had that "edge." That let me know he'd probably been into some other things—things that women like me should stay far away from.

One of my friends didn't find out until about ten years later, while I was grieving the loss of the love of my life, that she had said something about him that hurt my entire soul. Thinking back, it wasn't so much what she said, because there was some truth to it. However, the judgment and disdain behind her statement and the timing of it—while I was crying over the loss of Tony—was profound. Some of you are probably asking, why didn't you say something then? I couldn't. I valued the friendship more than my need to verbally cut her to the point that she wouldn't know she was bleeding. It's a good thing, too, because some of the most important aspects of my literary career came to fruition because of her assistance and input.

When I finally 'fessed up, she was shocked. "Why didn't you tell me?"

"Because I loved you enough that I needed you to stay in my life. The love was there, and I knew your heart."

Before I hit that judgment button on Tony, I realized that if I want to be taken for who, what, and where I am in life, then I had to start by doing the same in all of my relationships—intimate or otherwise. People go into relationships with that whole fixer-upper mentality. "When I clean him up, he'll be the perfect man," or "When he starts making those six figures, he'll be perfect for me." But so often, the truth is more along the lines that people are simply "as is." Take them or leave them, but don't try to "fix them," because when you do, then it ends up being one heck of an undertaking for everyone involved—especially if where you're trying to steer them is not part of their path or life's lesson. That leads to a whole lot of unnecessary pain and suffering. In the words of my dear sister, Sweet Brown, *Ain't nobody got time for that.*

But this—who *he* was—was a true test of my mettle.

Evidently, Tony had put out there in the Universe that he was ready for a change in his life. That request went up about the same time I had let loose with that angry little diatribe about having a placeholder, having unconditional love.

People, we had a match made in Hell? Heaven? ... well, in *something*. At the time, I wasn't quite sure.

To make matters worse, the chemistry between us was so strong, we couldn't hold a decent conversation unless we sat on opposite corners of a room. No getting around the physical attraction aspect of things. I couldn't run away if I tried. Oh, and I did try. Because I couldn't understand it. Bottom line? We were supposed to share time, space, and energy.

So for some reason, we were on the same spiritual trajectory. We both had a set of lessons to learn and evidently, we were the best two people in male and female form—with the right balance and chemistry—suited for the job. What did I ask for again? Oh, right. Unconditional love—from a placeholder.

A relationship that was supposed to be better than previous relationships, right?

Once, I had dated a guy for an entire year, and he was a direct reflection of what I felt about myself. The most chilling part was that he came over one night and said words that hurt me so badly, I didn't have another relationship for six years. "Black men don't like fat women. You're going to have to pay me for sex from now on."

He ended up in the hospital that night, but he was at my door pleading with me to take him back two months later. The damage had been done. I didn't want him. I didn't want *anyone!*

Mostly because of the pain from past liaisons, I don't go in for the games that people in relationships tend to play. I'm all up front. Lay the cards and your hand on the table, pick it up and run with it, or take your toys and go home. My intuition also lets me know when people try to play games. But of course, Tony had to try. That's what he was used to with women. Wanted them to make concessions for him just so they could hold on to a fine specimen of a handsome male who wasn't half-stepping when it came to the things a woman screams about.

So after making that initial connection—dynamic conversations over time, a powerful session of toe-curling, earth-shattering foreplay one night; life-altering, bar-raising love-making several days later—he's at a point where … "I got this. Yeah, I'm going to see how far I can push her; I'm going to see how I can get into her mind and take it over."

People, I let him roll right over that ego cliff all by himself. Didn't even slide him a rope to let him at least hang on for a few minutes before dropping off into the ocean.

In other words, because I didn't immediately give him what he wanted—which was to move into my place—he threw the typical male tantrum. I didn't hear from him for about a week.

Cool. In my mind, it was … "Well, the "placeholder" must have been all about getting the oil changed, a tune-up, an AC flush, new spark plugs, interior and exterior detailing, and the whole certified pre-owned vehicle overhaul. Fine with me."

If that was the way of teaching me a lesson about throwing requests out there with the wrong sentiment and energy—so be it. Lesson learned. *(Oh, but thanks for tightening a sister up in the process. High five. High five!). Whatever doesn't serve me, doesn't deserve me.*

But it wasn't over.

A week later, I received an unexpected call. And I could tell it took every ounce of effort for him to find that one humble bone in his body which allowed him to say, "If I let this thing between us go, if I let *you* go; I know I'll be making the worst mistake of my entire life."

In whatever form it's presented, I appreciate sincerity. I realized it took a lot for him to say just that and sum up his feelings. Did I go into, "Well, why didn't you call me?"—and add the classic sister girl neck rock? Did I make him sweat about it? *Well, let me think about it and get back to you.* No. What purpose would it serve? I don't play games. You lay it on the line—if I'm open, we're rolling. Try to manipulate me, I'm done, and *you're* rolling. If you come to me as a man and admit your mistake—there's no need for me to ride it into the ground. If I make a mistake, I own up to it. Apology accepted? Alrighty then. Not? I guess this is where I get off the train and let you ride the rest of the way without me.

One thing I never said to Tony was that in order to be with me he had to change—never implied it either. I accepted him for who he was. Evidently this was something *he* wanted, *he* needed for his soul's evolution. And he, with everything he brought to the table—which was purely himself—was exactly what I needed for my spiritual evolution. This created the perfect opportunity for spiritual growth, no matter what it looked like from the outside, or at any angle.

And things between us were simple. Sharing. Talking. Dreaming. All on equal footing, finding common ground and balance. Sharing what I learned in Temple.

Getting his point across to me was simple. "Baby, you know what you just did was illegal, right?"

After throwing him a curious look, I asked, "What?"

"That turn you made from the far lane and down 79th," he said, from the passenger seat. "You could get pulled over for that."

"Really?"

"Really. From now on, you need to slide up South Chicago, cut through the lot and *then* roll up 79th."

"All right."

Getting my point across was simple, too. Once when I prepared to get into the car, I paused for a moment, looked at him and said, "This is the last time that I open my car door when I'm with you."

A second later, he came around to the driver's side and held it while I slipped into the seat. When he made it back to the passenger side, he asked, "Suppose there's someone shooting at us? I'm supposed to hold it open for you then? When we should be breaking camp?"

I looked him square in the eyes. "If there's a bullet with my name on it, it'll catch me standing still. I'm not running. I prefer to meet my fate head on. I just hope they don't miss."

Tony stared at me for the longest time. End of discussion. Point taken. I never touched another car door again when we were together.

The amazing thing is, that's exactly how he died. A bullet. To the chest. On that night he had told his people, "Y'all won't see me for a while. I'm going to My Light. I'm going to my Comfort Zone." That is what he called me. *His Light. His Comfort Zone.* He never gave my name to any of his friends. I was his ...

sanctuary. The place he could come to when the world was giving him a swift kick in the rubber parts. The place where he could make sense of things that seemed pointless and endless.

The barrier between one part of his life and mine was also the main reason that I didn't find out he'd been killed until the day of his funeral. Correction—*after* his funeral had taken place. Killed by a man who he'd had an angry exchange of words with a few weeks before. A man who was upset about the amount of power Tony wielded. A man who was angry about the changes Tony was now making in his life. Positive changes they couldn't understand and didn't appreciate.

But oh, The Creator wanted me to know that Tony wasn't killed because he was involved in something he shouldn't be—because that was the first thing that crossed my mind. The thought had *stayed* in my mind.

I didn't know it then, but learned the day after his funeral, that the daughter of one of the women from my church was his friend. They had said she was "rough." I didn't know they meant *that* kind of "rough." When her mother passed me the phone, Kay said, "I can't talk to you in front of my mother, but I'm going to call you, all right? I have to talk to you. It wasn't what you think, all right?"

How the heck could she know what I was thinking?

Kay called the next night and said, "We *knew* it was a woman. We knew it was a woman! The kind of changes he was making—only a woman can have that kind of pull on a man. And that's all he was talking about, his Light; somebody he said was his Comfort Zone or something like that. Said that there were better things for us; that we didn't have to have a whole lot of money or education to reach our dreams and goals. We just had to try. We had to put it all down on paper, speak it into existence, then get out there and try. No excuses, no bull, balls to the wall …We could change our lives. We really could.

"You know when he got killed, we were going to _____

(I can't remember the restaurant she said) to celebrate. To put a toast up for what he was about to do."

That night, on the call with Kay, I found out that he had entered a program that accepted men with his type of past. They would get training and placement in higher paying jobs in the electrician's field. I had looked up the information for him when he asked, but I didn't know that he had actually gone through the process of getting in. He had called me earlier that day and told me he had great news and was coming to me that night to tell me.

"You know," Kay said. "We were out—sometimes at three, four in the morning—writing down our goals and stuff like that. Saying we were all getting out of the hood. All of us. He was talking to us about changing the way we think and how we look at things."

This was the point when the tears came. I never knew how much he'd absorbed of what I said to him. But to hear that he was trying to get the people around him to understand principles he had just learned from me was a powerful thing. That was what love felt like.

"I didn't think he really listened to me," I told Kay. "We were only together for a few months."

"Listen, if you were able to get him to change his life in two months, two days, twenty-four hours or whatever, and that was something nobody else could do in twenty-eight years—then that's what you were about. That's why he was with you."

Well, sum it up for me, why don't you?

"I'm glad he had a good woman in his life," Kay said. "Because he really was a great person."

She gave me several examples to illustrate her point, and I had an even greater appreciation for the man I thought I knew. Tony was a walking contradiction. But the truth of the matter is that it wasn't about me. These were changes *he* wanted to make. The Creator knew he was about to make that exit; but some things were needed *before* that happened: 1) a turbo jump from one type of consciousness to another; 2) to be an answer to a request I had put into the Universe; 3) to inspire those who were in his circle.

Kay took Tony's advice and did what he'd encouraged her to do. She's now married, has three children and a degree—one of the goals and dreams she wrote down one of the mornings they were out in the streets.

The Creator sent me someone who I felt was totally "out of character", but it ended up being my best relationship. At least to date. He needed to have the right blend of everything—strength, experiences, and background included—to provide whatever lessons came from me laying that request on so thick. *Placeholder until a real number comes along.*

I'll always have your back.

Maybe The Creator was a little upset with me for snapping the way I had; or maybe the experience was all about showing me that my prayers and requests are always answered, even if the answer is, "No" or "Not right now" or "Hold on, it's coming". That interlude showed me that I needed to stop thinking things had to come in a way that I'd have total control over, or that it would look, taste, touch, smell, and sound a certain way.

Tony had one simple request: to shower with him. And I couldn't do it. That was when I realized that The Creator had sent me a wonderful, amazing man who loved me for me, but I didn't love me for me. The greatest lesson of all was that love started and ended with me. And loving yourself will attract someone who loves you too—in the raw form. Makeup or no makeup, slender or like me. I'm a plus-size woman, and that means the person needs to love rolls and cellulite. Basically, they'll love all four cheeks and a couple of chins.

The lessons from Tony have echoed with me for all this time. As a "placeholder," it was a starting point for realizing that

I had to release a lot more. But more importantly, I needed to love myself more. Though I had done some healing work, I needed to love myself *unconditionally* before I could think about forming my lips to speak or poising my fingers to place another tall order of a request to The Creator about having a mate.

Indeed. The Creator sent me Tony as an answer to prayer. I definitely consider that having my back.

Chapter 9

YOU REAP WHAT YOU SOW

Karma or reaping what one sows has played an important part in my life. This part of my story comes with a little Bible commentary first that ties in a bit with what I wrote about earlier.

Before writing this book, my favorite person in the Bible was David? Why? Because David was honest about his sins; he loved to have a great time. But no matter how much dirt he did, he loved The Creator, always gave respect where respect was due. And he still managed to be the apple of God's eye and continued to be blessed.

So let me get this straight; kill off the husband of the woman we want to marry; eat, drink—a lot—and be merry and *still* come out on top? Well, sign me up for that program. Yes, indeed.

Where I fell out of love with David was in writing this book. That's when I realized he was like my father, uncle, and the men who had damaged me in my current life. David didn't value his daughter at all. He also didn't value someone else's daughter.

I can respect his spiritual walk, but doing research for this book made me feel some kind of way when I equated *my* walk with Tamar's—a king's daughter, who should have been loved and protected.

David seemed to always have things go his way. But let's look at things from several perspectives—the things that took him off his square. Now, let's go back to that "scandal" mentioned in the earlier part of this book. David was walking on the roof of his palace as he did every evening, saw Bathsheba taking a bath, and in typical kingly, male fashion, he said, "I want her." On the flipside, we have to think about the fact that people back in those days were modest, and walking around naked wasn't exactly the "in" thing. Sooooo, there's a possibility that Bathsheba timed things correctly, putting herself out there on purpose so she could catch David's eye, seduce him, and trade up a husband. Or he was setting that prime example for his son of *I want it, I have the power, and I can have it.*

Now mind you, David wasn't short in the female department. He had a slew of wives and concubines already. But he still had Bathsheba summoned to his place and they did the doggone thing. I mean, how could she refuse being with the king?

No problem.

Then, she got pregnant.

Big problem.

At the time, Uriah, Bathsheba's husband, was off fighting a war for David. So, if hubby wasn't there to do the honors ... then who was the baby's daddy? David quickly tried to cover things up by bringing hubby home to hurry up and get it on with Bathsheba. Then the baby could be born under the "cover" of their marriage bed and David would be off the hook.

Well, here's where things became interesting. Hubby didn't do as he was commanded. Instead, he slept inside the walls of the palace with his men rather than go home to his wife. Kind of makes me wonder if that's the reason Bathsheba was so ripe for the plucking in the first place. But I digress. Hubby was actually following an ancient kingdom rule applying to warriors in active service. So, he gets a pass.

Several times, hubby doesn't follow David's orders that would put him in bed with the wife in enough time for the baby to "officially" be considered the hubby's. So, what's a not-so-secret lover to do? A lover with the type of power David had? He sends Uriah off to war again. This time he makes sure old boy is on the frontline so the enemy will do David's dirty work and kill off Uriah. That sounds like some *Scandal, How to Get Away With Murder,* or *Game of Thrones* type of stuff to me.

The plan worked, and David married Bathsheba and moved her into the palace. Happy times, right?

Even though David was the "apple of God's eye" and all that, The Creator was not pleased with what he'd done. That was some low-down dirty stuff up in there, up in there. First rule when you're about to do some dirt is that if you can't do it all yourself, then make sure the cast of characters who know everything remains small. David thought he had covered all the bases. Only a few people knew the real deal: a) the messenger he sent to Bathsheba's house to bring her to the palace for a little slap and a lot of tickle, b) the general he used to put Uriah on the front line, and c) Bathsheba herself.

Here's the thing: The Creator knew and because David was full of himself and wasn't listening to his angels, ancestors, or his own self-accusing spirit, the point had to be brought home in a different way.

The Creator had given David so, so much. Had taken him from being a lowly shepherd boy to being a powerful king.

And *this* was how he returned all that favor? *This* was what happened when he became a top dog? Seriously? No, no, my brother, you won't get off that easily. Let me bring that lesson in a way you will never forget.

The prophet Nathan came to David and told him the parable of the rich man who took away the one little ewe lamb of his poor neighbor, and the story made David angry. So Nathan hit him with a zinger by comparing the story to what David had done with Uriah and Bathsheba. David was instantly remorseful and confessed his sin. Bathsheba's child by David was struck with a severe illness and died a few days after birth. David accepted that as his punishment.

Yes, there was now a king in the land, and that was supposed to mean what happened during the time when the Levite hurled the pieces of his concubine to the twelve tribes to stir the pot should have been a thing of the past, right? When push came to shove, David did not handle the business of how his daughter had been treated. Instead, he threw up his hands and shrugged. He valued his son's needs and misdeeds over his daughter's emotional, mental, and physical wellbeing. The same way he valued what he wanted, even going so far as breaking two of the commandments by coveting another man's wife, impregnating her, then having the husband killed to cover up that misdeed.

Amnon didn't even bother to cover his wickedness. After getting what he wanted, he simply kicked Tamar to the curb as if she were yesterday's trash. Didn't care what would happen to her because nothing would happen to him. He knew it. His father had already given in to that unusual request, which made him complicit.

With the story of the Levite's concubine in my book *Transition*, the text repeated that there was "no king in the land". The Israelites compounded one sin after the other, and the women and children were the unfortunate recipients of bad judgment on all sides.

Now, because "the king in the land" allowed Absalom's sister to be disrespected and cast aside, Absalom handled the business himself, then made plans to take over David's territory and declare himself as king. What better way to show "who's the man" than by having sex with ten of David's women? David slept with *one* woman. His son slept with *ten*. And he did it ... drum roll please ... in public. Sex with ten women out in the open. See, I knew those Bible types were getting it in back then. Now you know David wasn't going to take that lying down (no pun intended). This led to a rebellion that plunged the kingdom into war.

Sleeping with Uriah's wife, trying to cover it up, and killing off the husband had repercussions that far outweighed the loss of their child born of a murderous and adulterous liaison. Several lives were lost in that first war, and then in the war that transpired long after. David's kingdom, family, and friends were in an uproar—all stemming from one selfish and ego-driven incident.

So, how could he have put a stop to his son's off-putting request to have a private interlude with his half-sister? David was an intelligent man. Everything that Amnon asked was out of order. It *had* to be Tamar. Not a servant. It *had* to be in his chambers. It *had* to be that she fixed that food in his presence and fed him from her hands. Come on now. When I was growing up, parents said do as I say, not as I do. But David didn't even put Amnon in check verbally.

David saw the signs and ignored them. Like father, like son. Consequences be damned.

At the beginning of David's life, he was more in control of the flow; directing it, following his inner spirit, and what The Creator had lined up for him. All good things came his way.

After the incident with Uriah and Bathsheba, where he let dark consciousness take his life for a test drive, David's family was out of control. After Amnon raped his sister, Tamar, David's handling of things caused Absalom to seek revenge and later come back in an attempt to overthrow the kingdom. David lost both sons because of his actions and technically his daughter, too.

My editor, Janice Allen, author of Growth which is in this Merry Hearts Series, had this to say about this part of the book:

I respect that David might no longer be your favorite character. But we can't throw him under the bus, because he still found favor in God's eyes and was a man after God's own heart (1 Samuel 14:13)—in spite of his shortcomings. His life was a portrait of success and failure (the same success and failure we all struggle with), and the Biblical record highlights the fact that David was far from perfect (as we are).

We do a disservice to ourselves when we point only at his flaws, because we miss the lesson that we can learn about our own lives (the most important being that a Perfect God has chosen to love us Imperfect People in spite of ourselves). So let's be mindful of dragging him through the mud, because at the same time we may be missing the opportunity to teach something about our shortcomings and God's love.

All in all, it seemed that David was more tossed and turned by the events happening within his life than being in the driver's seat as he once had been. He was reacting to things that happened, rather than taking things in command as he had previously always done—because he had lost that connection with The Creator.

Through all that had transpired, Bathsheba gave birth to Solomon, who would succeed his father to the throne despite the fact that there was another child next in line after Absalom had been killed. Solomon became known as the world's wisest man and he wasn't half-stepping either. What was he into … like 700 wives and 300 concubines? Some of them were his father's. Busy man. Busy man. Although both men had their strong points and their flaws; but they equally had the greatest impact on the history we find in the Bible.

What does all of this tell us? The most powerful outcomes can start with the most interesting of circumstances. But everything we do, good, great, bad, or ugly, sets the stage for what comes back to us.

If we don't live in our purpose, or listen to that still, small voice—or whisper, as Oprah calls it—then we're not in the driver's seat. We're letting life happen *to* us instead of letting it happen *for* us. Now you know at some point, that still small voice whispered to David, "You'd better leave that man's woman alone." But his ego answered that little directive with, "But *I'm* the king. I'm running things up in this camp. I can have all the women I want and then some." *Hmmmm. Where did Amnon get that from?*

And how did that work out for him?

"God gives his sunlight to both the evil and the good, and He sends rain on the just and the unjust alike," Matthew 5:45

So let's talk about Karma for a minute. It is the sum of a person's actions in the current and previous states of existence, viewed as deciding their fate in future existences. To reap what you sow is harvesting what you conceived. Whenever most people talk about Karma or Reaping, they're referring to only the bad things because that's what makes the most impact and stays fresh in the mind. Sometimes, we think people who have done us wrong don't seem to be getting *their* share of it, like we're getting ours.

Not so. They do.

Karma. There's the good kind. There's the bad kind. But you know what we remember most? The kind that comes with a calling card that says, "Remember that stuff you did? Well, you placed a full order of payback—and heeeeeeeeere it is." Then wham! "The stuff" starts rolling downhill, and you're not able to get out of its path before it lays you flat on your back. The minute you try to get up and dust off, then—Wham! Another one hits.

You might ask yourself, "What did I do to deserve this? I'm a good person; I don't do anyone any type of wrong. Why is all this happening to me?"

But the bigger question we ask when we're catching it is, "Why do others get off so easy when they should be catching it too?"

Remember, you're not with that person every waking moment. So you don't know how it hits them. You're not privy to every single thing that's happening in their lives. You only see the surface. You only see it through your pain-stained lens. You can't know a person's inner pain and struggle. They only can see yours because when they flex and inflict pain, you react. Then we start taking notes and comparing. They hurt me; harmed me; but they don't look any worse for wear.

The Creator will revisit their efforts in due time and can handle it a lot better than you ever could. Let's take my father for instance. I could *never* have inflicted the type of pain and suffering he caused me. He laid in that hospital bed for more than two months, in pain, couldn't move a muscle, couldn't blink his eyes, his entire body paralyzed from head to toe— but his mind was totally active and aware of everything going around him. I could never have done that. But it happened. And for some reason The Creator knew it needed to happen where I could see it.

But life doesn't always work like that.

Here's the kick in the rubber parts; I felt no joy in seeing my father that way. Not a single ounce of pleasure from seeing him suffer. Why? Because that's not who I am. Reveling in someone else's pain or misfortune is of dark consciousness. It's almost childish in the sense that you want to stick out your tongue and say, "Nah. That's what you get. You shouldn't have done that to me." That might have felt great when we were children and didn't know any better, but now—really? Is that what we're about? No, I don't think so.

That incident with my father showed that The Creator always has a way of taking care of things. Including people who have hurt or harmed me. Because then it is about the other person's lessons that have been brought on by what they have signed up for and what they've done to others. It's not me getting all up in the mix and trying to figure out what I can do to them to pay them back; to inflict as much pain on them as they have on me.

All in all, The Creator takes care of the things that need to be taken care of—for you, me, our families, friends, enemies, total strangers—everyone. You don't have to see it in order to know that it works.

Just believe that it does.

Chapter 10

Number One Son

Now here's where I know I'm on the path to manifesting healthier relationships. My son was home from college and I thought he needed a little shaking up in order to get him on a more productive path. Part of the issue was a lesson in sweat equity—when you're not contributing as much to a household financially, you can give it by doing more around the house. He was not feeling that. And I wasn't feeling the fact that he wasn't feeling that.

On a day I had to take out the garbage and do the dishes, I made a decision to have peace on my birthday. That was my present to myself. My action, in my mind, was *totally* correct. But the timing of it was all wrong. On the coldest day in decades, when cars were frozen and stuck on Lake Shore Drive, I packed his things and had them waiting for him when he came home. I let him know he could take the suitcase right now or come back with a truck and get it all at once.

This was the first time we ever had a break in our relationship.

Just a few weeks ago, he was in Costco and I called him with the video feature on and asked him to call me back when he had a moment. He said he did right then. I apologized to him for putting him out of the house that bitterly cold day so long ago. I confessed that while it was the right thing to do, it was the absolute wrong time.

"I don't want to leave this earth without giving you the apology you deserve," I told him.

He said, "Come on, Mom. Don't have me crying in Costco." But he did shed a tear or two right then and there! Then, he said, "I forgave you for that a long time ago."

Two weeks later, a video call came in from him while I was at home and he wanted to talk. Evidently, his beloved had a little "come to Jesus meeting with him". And it ended with him understanding exactly what I meant all those years ago, so he apologized to me. And I said, "Come on, son. Don't have me crying in Costco."

Those words are now an inside joke for us.

In my other book in the series, *Transition*, I share how his encouragement helped me release the anger and resentment I held for his father. So many blessings came to both of us because I listened to him.

One profound recurring dream had a message for me and I didn't understand the meaning until my son shared something.

The world as we knew it was about to end, and everyone here had to leave to slide into another dimension. The issue was that we had to leave by way of an Olympic sized pool and it was necessary to breathe in a certain manner.

For the entire dream, I was afraid to approach the pool and go into the water. Until the freeze came and I had no choice.

Everything in this place was freezing over and there would be no amount of heat that would keep me warm.

I had that dream multiple times and finally in one of those dreams, I did not know if I made it to wherever that other dimension was supposed to be. But after this same dream for years, it was a monumental effort to get over the fear and take that first step to go into the pool and try.

Here's where the dream was profound. I told my son the dream the moment I felt relieved that it had finally come to what I thought was the end. And here's what shows connectedness. Unknown to me, he's always had the other half of the dream of us coming up in this cave and people pulling us out of the water. He never understood his part of the dream. But as many years as I had the dream and never told anyone, when I finally did, the answer I needed came from another source. I haven't had that dream again since, but it also put in context what he'd been dreaming all those years.

Message: Getting over my fear. And his understanding that everything would be fine.

Some of our mother-son experiences are tucked inside my novels *Loving Me for Me* and *She Touched My Soul*, and his novels: Superwoman's Child: *Son of a Single Mother*, *The Things I Could Tell You!*, and his current one—*Knight of Irondale*.

Chapter 11

Six Low

Another positive male influence showed up in my life. Since we reconnected, I have learned a great deal from my nephew. DeMarco was thirty-six then, and the last time we'd spoken to, or seen, him was at age twelve. Before my son left for another university in South Carolina, we located my nephew by finding his grandparents' house on the Southeast side. It was a wonderful day for all of us.

Connecting with him helped with something else. I had always wanted to play Bid Whist. The card game seemed like the "grown up" thing to do. My family was a Spades game family, but on those church trips we took down South to Canton, Mississippi with the choir, that's when I witnessed Bid Whist players in action. Learning before then proved a bit challenging because some players were too competitive, too serious, and much too impatient to teach someone the ropes.

Could almost make folks lose their religion, as much cussing, drinking, and smoking as they were doing … but I digress.

My nephew is a champion Bid Whist player. There's one reason he reached that status. When DeMarco sits at a table, he *expects* to win each and every time. It's in his walk, "trash" talk, and his demeanor. Ninety percent of the time when he plays, he *does* win.

One Friday night around eight, he called and said, "Auntie, come out and play Bid Whist with me."

He wanted me to visit a place I now call the shark tank—a spot on 64th & Stony Island in Chicago where a group of seasoned card players get together to play Bid Whist, chow down, listen to good music, and have a great time. My initial reaction was, "No." Those people had been playing for years—they were tournament players. At the time, I was nowhere near their league. Well, he twisted my arm, forcing me to go after saying, "Come on. Just for an hour, Auntie."

We came through the door kicking tail and taking names. When we arrived it was nine, but we didn't get up from that first table until midnight. And that was because another team *finally* beat us. He walked me over to the buffet table and fixed me a plate. We ate and were back down at another table. I forgot all about that "only one hour" statement.

For the most part, I had let DeMarco take the lead in playing all night long—because I was intimidated and afraid to fail. But I finally landed a hand that was so dynamic, I was afraid *not* to bid. My nephew would've never let me live it down if I had passed on a hand like that. So, I bid a six low to take out a five no trump. Bid Whist players understand that's a smart move. There were two gaps in my spread that I knew would land me in trouble. We played out the hand, and when I entered the "trouble" zone, my nephew whipped out the cards that mattered and slapped them on the table.

When the last book turned, DeMarco jumped up from the

table and yelled, "Six, Low. Boston. And she did it by her damn self."

Actually, I couldn't have done it without him, but I took his meaning.

All of a sudden, people in the room—about fifty spread out around six tables and a couple of sofas—applauded.

I smiled, though I didn't understand why there would have been a reason for them to do that—my kind of win happened for them all the time.

But it was my nephew being proud of me that did it for them and me. After that, I started bidding more and more—making most, losing a few. But I had the will to try; releasing the fear of not being good enough. Releasing my normal way of embracing failure first, then found that jumping into the deep end wasn't as bad as I thought it would be.

Susan Peters, one of my literary clients, hosted a party at her home. Sure enough, there came a call for people who could play Bid Whist. I reluctantly raised my hand, but immediately put them on notice that I was a "rookie." There were a few groans, as expected. They weren't rookies, but no one else wanted to play with them to make it a foursome—two players against another two. Spades and Bid Whist players can be brutal.

My partner and I *clowned*. Boston no-trump; Boston from the low end; Boston from the high end. For those of you who don't play the game, suffice it to say those are great things. It's when a team has all of the cards/books, and the opposing team has none. Soon the game went so sour that our opponents tossed the cards on the table and didn't want to play anymore. One of them glared at me as he left the table and said, "She lied to us. She ain't no damn rookie."

That right there put me on notice. When I told them that, it was to lower their expectations of what I would be able to do. In other words, I had already set myself up for failure before even playing the game.

All that year with my nephew was about learning to play from the best and with the best. For some reason, it never crossed my mind that I had absorbed the strategies and habits of people who had played the cream of the crop for years. So telling others and myself that I was a rookie was as far from the truth as I could get.

No matter your life's circumstances, try to continuously surround yourself with loving, caring people—people who are about something; people who want more out of life than just working a nine-to-five, collecting a check, retiring, and then moseying off into the sunset. I mean, where's the fun in that?

Know that throwing in your cards because the ones you were dealt don't seem quite fair is not the way to go. So when it comes to applying this same knowledge to all aspects of your life, you might not want to tell anyone you're a rookie at anything; especially since The Creator has given you the tools, resources, and people in your life so you can set yourself up to be a champion at everything.

Chapter 12

SHIFTING MY PARADIGM

At one point in my writing career, I wanted to write stronger male characters. The first one in *More Than Enough* was a man who only became stronger when two women put him through a male training program because they wanted to share him. (Yes, I started off writing *those* kind of books. So stop giving me the side-eye). The next one, in *She Touched My Soul*, was a man who was on the brink of spiraling into addiction before a mysterious woman entered his life and started him on a different path. Then with *Every Woman Needs a Wife*, the male was unfaithful and it was all about him changing his ways to win his wife back.

From that point, I wanted to write stronger alpha male characters as my lead. My thoughts were that we have enough of the other kind floating around in real life. So I refuse to put Beta, Gamma, or Delta men in print unless they are supporting or walk-on characters, never the lead. Interestingly enough, when the decision was made, I was thirty-nine and personally didn't have enough to draw on to actually write that strong alpha male.

The Creator solved that problem for me in a miraculous way. I had always thought the most beautiful words a woman could hear from a mate was, "I love you." No, not so much. How about the words: "I never knew what peace was until I met you."

Let tell you, when he said that, my drawers dropped to my ankles and ran to the curb!

People say "I love you" all the time, and most haven't given any real thought to what it truly means to love unconditionally. That means it isn't conditioned on the other person doing or being what you expect; it isn't even conditioned on them returning that love.

Those ten words from Tony will resonate with me for the rest of my life, along with the lessons I learned by being with him.

Those lessons were so profound that I realize he was only in my life for that short time to prepare me for the "real thing." Prepare me, so I wasn't bringing so much baggage—three suitcases, a carry-on, and a trunk—into the next intimate relationship.

The experience prepared me to stop demanding things from The Creator and recognize they will slide into my life when it's time. So I don't have a need to say: "I'd like him short, sunburnt, smart, and sensational; tall, tan, tantalizing, and terrific; or butterscotch, sexy, intelligent, and full of fire." Yes, those are all superficial things. I want peace, harmony, joy, adventure, compassion, balance, and a host of other wonderful attributes. I want to experience these, and leave The Creator to handle the details of the when, what, where, who, and how.

Another thing I'll share about Tony. Loving him helped

me to love myself more. In my novel *Open Door Marriage*, the lead male is Dallas, and the lead female character is Alicia. Dallas asks Alicia to take a shower with him and she refuses because she is self-conscious about her body, and even more self-conscious about her love for him—a younger man. Dallas takes matters into his own hands. In real life, the experience was a wake-up call for me.

For two years, I had asked The Creator to send me a man who would love me for me. But the moment I couldn't step into the shower with Tony was when I realized that *he* loved me for me, but *I* didn't love me for me.

Now that I can write about the real thing—I mean love—I can also manifest it. So since my time with him ended in an untimely way, I've focused on having a love affair with myself. I haven't written another list of what I'd like to experience in a relationship. For a long time, I didn't ask The Creator to send me another mate. No, my wake-up call was a startling example of the fact that I need to love me for me. So, I've spent time learning how to do exactly that. And I'm going to be honest; it has not been an easy task. Saying that I love me is easy. Showing it is another boat to row. But I'm working on it every single day. And there are people in my corner helping me to achieve success in those areas.

Who's in my corner?

Spiritual Corner - Sesvalah, Debra, Janice, Janine, Ehryck, J. L., Pastor Karen, La Ammitai, and Tribe

Family Corner - my true mother, J. L., Sesvalah, Janice, DeMarco, Jennifer, Debra, Tribe

Health Corner –My FB friends who do those Mermaid challenges with me, Tribe

Financial Corner - Debra, Sesvalah, Ehryck, (I should say J. L. since he's hit this corner more often than I would like; but this is all about who contributes *to* the corner—with people who consistently hold my vision of prosperity, or give information/ advice that leads to prosperity; or actually contribute dollars.)

Intimate Corner - ***crickets*** But I know he's coming.

And truthfully, before the time of this writing, I haven't asked The Creator to send me another mate because I'm still loving on myself. Part of that experience has been learning about non-sexual touch. Some might jump to the conclusion that this is some sort of orgy, but sex, or anything resembling it, isn't even allowed. A cuddle party is a gathering where people learn to discern the touch they want from the touch they don't. A strict guideline in cuddle parties is that you don't have to allow anyone you don't want in your physical space.

Anyone who wants to touch, embrace, or caress you at a cuddle party must ask your permission every step of the way. Just because I allowed you to touch my hand, doesn't mean you have permission to touch my arm. You have to ask.

If the recipient is unsure whether they want you to touch them, you must treat that as a no. And when you say no, the other person has to respond with, "Thank you for taking care of yourself."

This awareness of my right to set boundaries changed my whole dynamic. When I went back to church, my answer became no to certain people I felt uncomfortable getting an embrace from. Some thought I was a little strange because I was now respecting my space and wanted others to respect it too. That whole turn to your neighbor thing and give them a hug? That's a thing of the past.

See, when we were children, we weren't given the opportunity to say no. We were told to hug auntie so and so, or kiss uncle whatchamacallit. We weren't given ownership of our bodies; just had to do as we were told. When children feel some kind of way towards an adult—listen! Don't force them to hug and kiss people if they don't want to do so. My niece wrote a book, *Lady of Jeffrey Manor*, and it included a profound statement from Lena Sledge: *The days of children sitting at the same table with the people who have molested them are over!*

When we first come into being, we're not taught to own our bodies and ourselves. We belong to the adults. They tell us what to do, what not to do, and sometimes the things we don't want to do.

We don't want vegetables, we still have to eat them anyway. Don't want to go to bed, but we have a curfew, and there's no choice. Because everyone else rules us.

As we grow and take ownership of our bodies, and realize we dictate what does and does not happen, we begin to know what we want and it also helps identify more about the things we need.

Now we're old enough to know who we want on our bodies and in our bodies, and we can own that "No." And we express that love on our own terms.

Later, as we become more aware, we ask for respect, love, appreciation, compassion, and what we want to experience in the relationship and it's not so much about the person. It's the experience that is packaged in the right physical component.

In the same way you're careful what you put in your body—and I mean meal choices, that should also go for who you accept *into* your body, and that means love choices.

In my earlier list of people in my corners, did you notice how some people appeared in more than one corner? Most times that's the case. People play more than one role in your life. And notice how some people should probably be in more than one corner, but didn't quite make it.

Same way that I declutter my home every three months, revisiting that list is on the plate as well. It's always interesting to see how things and people shift.

You can do the same thing. Take out a sheet of paper and make a list of the people who are in your corners—family corner, spiritual corner, health corner, financial corner, intimate corner. People who have an impact in your life make the list, not ones who are just "holding ground" or "taking up space". These are the people who matter the most. People who help you with your life lessons while you're on the earth scene.

Next, let's talk about the lightning list (flow of energy—the givers and takers). In your life, there are some people who understand balance. Then there are those who take and take and take and don't even realize you're giving. The one-sided relationship where you're the one doing all the work of making it work.

A little exercise learned in a workshop helps me figure out what's what. Why don't you try it for yourself?

Make a circle on a sheet of paper. Write your name in the center. Then write along the outside of the circle the names of the people who you interact with most (positive and negative). Now put an arrow from you to those you give your energy to. Make the arrow thicker or thinner according to how much energy you give. Now draw another arrow from them to you (thicker or thinner) according to how much energy they give back.

If you're noticing that in some cases the flow of energy is off (not an even exchange), those are the relationships that bear looking into. Those are the relationships that need to be shifted or changed—could be your family, children, friends, etc. I'm not saying kick anyone to the curb; but building a different relationship or a more harmonious and balanced experience might be a good thing for your peace of mind.

And as Sean Connery said in The Untouchables, "Herein lies the lesson."

Chapter 13

FINDING YOUR PURPOSE

What is the one thing you would do even if you wouldn't get paid for it? Now on a base level, whatever that is, might not be what helps you keep an address (pay the bills), so what you're passionate about, what your purpose is, and what is profitable, might not all be the same things. At least, not in the beginning.

Sometimes your purpose will find you.

I did not grow up saying I want to be an author. With everything that happened, I simply wanted to exist— peacefully, without any more people hurting me. My mother, father, and uncle had done enough to start with, and it was all I could do to finally embrace a path that would put me on the way to healing.

Writing became my passion, but only later as I helped others use writing as a path to healing did I realize it was my purpose. I actually had a numerology blueprint done by La Ammitai, and it confirmed my purpose as a spiritual messenger. Spiritual, not religious. Because to be honest, I've done the religious chitlin' circuit trying to find answers, and I've been through a number of religions and denominations—Baptist, Methodist, Apostolic (for one day because when I didn't receive the gift of tongues from being in that Tarry Room for five hours, they said, according to their doctrine, I wasn't saved and I felt lost and untethered), then Ausar Auset, Nation of Islam.

One of the editors of this book was so hurt by reading this part of my story that she sent these words in an email right before this went to press:

"Many years ago when that church told you that you were not saved because you couldn't speak in tongues, they planted a seed of mistrust toward God (why would He require tongues and then not help me speak in tongues, knowing how earnestly I tried). Speaking in tongues is indeed one of the gifts of God, but He does not give it to everyone. He does not require anyone to operate in what He hasn't given in order to prove that you're saved. Here's how you know you are saved Romans10:9-10:

9: That if thou shalt confess with thy mouth the Lord Jesus, and shalt believe in thine heart that God hath raised him from the dead, thou shalt be saved.
10: For with the heart man believeth unto righteousness; and with the mouth confession is made unto salvation.

You, my dear friend, are saved.

The Baha'i Faith is the only religion I found that values women the same as men. When I embraced spirituality and that connection to The Creator, Mother-Father God, the Source, some may call it the Universe, or All That Is, that's when I found exactly what I had been searching for—understanding, peace, contentment, purpose. Everything else falls in line—passion and determination; purpose and contentment; prosperity and abundance.

The more I fell into this literary life and my purpose, the more it provided an opportunity for growth that gave me a sense of peace and contentment.

In the years since Tony was taken from this earth, my writing changed greatly because now I could write what I *had* experienced instead of what I *wanted* to experience. I've written around thirty books, some of them reliving that awesome experience with the love of my life. I write for others to understand the lessons I've learned.

Thank you for taking this journey with me, the transition from being forgotten to forgiven and highly favored. It is my hope that something within these pages helped to inspire you in some way. And you might want to take a gander at some of the other books I penned that deal with particular issues.

My Time in the Sun: Combined stories from the backgrounds of my sister and two nieces.

Loving Me for Me: The novel that shows no matter the cultural background or physical appearance ... love is an inside job.

Open Door Marriage: First story that I wrote that used Tony as a main character.

She Touched My Soul: The novel is where I learned to forgive my mother.

Was it Good For You Too? The novel where I explored the question: Where was God when all of these horrible things happened?

King of Durabia: My spiritual journey and finding love in the most unlikely places.

King of Devon: The novel that was part of a Tribe challenge for me to put love on the page and believe in it again.

In every novel I write, there is something of my pain, pleasure, growth and spiritual journey. This is why I write.

To end this book, I'm sharing a few of the affirmations that I've used.

I Am thankful for allowing others to have their life experiences, and I support them fully in their process. I am totally at peace and non-judgmental with their path and outcomes.

I Am thankful for more loving and harmonious relationships in all aspects of my life.

I Am thankful that my body is slimming down, releasing excess pounds and inches in ease, comfort, and joy, under grace, and in a perfect way. Exercising and dancing is easy and effortless, and my metabolism speeds up to accommodate this desire.

I Am thankful that I receive lots of abundance and prosperity from expected and unexpected sources on a daily basis. I am experiencing a superabundance of prosperity and people to help me, places, things, and events, money, substance, and health of my projects and myself.

I Am thankful that my old/outstanding accounts payable, bills, debts to people and companies, are paid in full at very little or no cost to me, under grace and in a perfect way.

I Am thankful for my physical body, my cells, my atoms, my molecules, my lymphatic system, my digestive system, my circulatory system, my nervous system, my brain, my heart, my organs, my emotional body, my spiritual body, my mind, and my connection to The Creator.

And this is a little of what I wrote when I asked The Creator for a mate and Tony came: I Am experiencing a wonderful, harmonious, peaceful and balanced intimate relationship where I am protected, cherished, and loved by a man who protects my heart, mind, and body, who comforts and uplifts me; who is adventurous, spontaneous, focused, supportive, compassionate, inclusive, sharing, giving, fair, complementary, trusting, and trustworthy.

You know, when I was with the man who was the first love of my life, my vibration changed and it seemed I started attracting various kinds of men.

All of a sudden, I would walk down the street on my way to work, and men who had never spoken to me before, were smiling and speaking. In my mind's eye I was like, *when I was single, I couldn't get nothing—nada—zilch, but now that I'm with someone, men were showing me all kinds of love.*

Manifesting your soul mate begins with the love you give yourself, then you'll be in alignment to attract the person to show you that kind of love. Have a love affair with yourself, shower yourself and your vibration will be open and receptive for others to love you too.

That's a whole lot of pressure for you to put on someone else, to shore up the parts you feel you're missing. Fill in those parts, start treating you like you want them to treat you.

When you finally encounter the person for you, trust me, it will make up for all the years of famine, and it will be feasting time.

Remember, I've stated that I wrote and spoke my intentions for two years before I manifested the man who was the love of my life. I had asked for a placeholder until the real number came along.

Let me tell you, on a scale from one to ten, that man was a day-um. And that man put me back to factory settings. Before, my heart was hurt by the men who were supposed to love me.

He was worth the wait. Almost made me wish I was a virgin all over again, but if that were the case, I wouldn't know how good it was.

Pull out a few sheets of paper. Write down the negative experiences—past and present—that have impacted you the most. One line each will suffice. Right next to those experiences, write a single word or words to describe what you were feeling at the time. After you're done, pull out another sheet of paper and rewrite those experiences into a positive affirmation.

If one experience made you angry, you might write something like: I Am experiencing an overabundance of joy (or happiness).

Do this for every single experience. There might be some duplicates, but remember to write the affirmations in present tense—by starting it with "I Am experiencing."

Another thing I learned, is that anxiety starts the night before. Instead of going to sleep with the cares and worries of the world on your mind and shoulders, say what you're grateful for. Name something wonderful that has happened to you throughout your day. Leave those worries to The Creator to work everything out. Start each day with gratitude. Before you pick up the phone. Before you jump on social media. Before you set foot out of bed. Gratitude.

My day starts with: I am grateful for excellent health and strength. I am grateful for peace of mind and prosperity. I am grateful for all things great and small. I am grateful for my son and Donisha (his fiancée at the time of this writing) ... then I go down the list of Tribe and all of my spiritual corner, family, and this sets the tone for my day.

I can't tell you how important that is because you'll encounter all kinds of energies and people throughout your day. Well, it became so toxic on my job that a co-worker went completely off on one of the attorneys. When I offered to help him, she went off on me too. So I told her, "I don't know where you purchased your attitude, but you need to return it for a full refund and get back on your meds." She walked away, came back an hour later and apologized to the attorneys, then to me. I accepted her embrace and she said, "Girl, you know the Devil is busy." My thoughts? *Yes, he's busy using you.*

Begin and end your day with gratitude and maybe folks won't think you got up on the wrong side of the bed or that you haven't had enough coffee. I'm just saying!

Today is your Independence Day. Why not declare your independence from the things that might be holding you captive? It is equally important that you undertake the journey for spiritual, physical, mental, and emotional health as well. By stating your personal affirmations in the morning and right before you go to bed, soon you'll be able to feel a sense of peace as you release yourself along with everyone and everything involved.

Ask me how I know.

Chapter 13

NK's Tribe Called Success

And then there is Tribe. *My* Tribe. Some of the biggest lessons I've learned come from them. They are my balance, my voice of reason, the place I go to vent and find comfort and understanding. They understand me because my life is wrapped up in this literary thing.

Each one of them is important, but I have a pretty interesting issue in that there are only 3 men in the Tribe. One of the men is on the outskirts, but he is supportive of all the tribe. Given my history with men, I've found that they don't come at me the right way as clients, sliding in my direct messages as though the world—specifically I—owe them something. Hence more women are in the Tribe than men. Shakir is the Tribe husband. My son is the Tribe son/brother. Both of them carry the balance of male energy for the women of the Tribe. Ehryck is the Tribe life coach, as well as a celebrity life coach.

The most powerful takeaway from Ehryck, the author of *Act As If: The Secret Power of Your Thoughts*, is that when you say I Am, you are making a contract with The Creator. So I'm learning to be careful of the statements that come behind the words I Am. Even in jest because what if that's what I manifest in my life?

When I came up with the idea for this series, it was because a great deal of our series had not been something our Christian fiction authors could take part in. Merry Hearts came to mind for us to do something inspirational. Even this was a lesson. I had put the idea on the back burner, but I slid into a room on Clubhouse one day and was verbally spanked by a prophetess who read me up and down about not doing what The Creator told me to do. So the Tribe kicked this into high gear. The Merry Hearts series was supposed to include twelve books, but ended up with nine.

Each series we have birthed, Kings of the Castle, Knights of the Castle, Queens of the Castle, The Pleasure Series, and Merry Hearts, has given me a spiritual lesson in self-growth and inner reflection. Every member of the Tribe is a reflection of myself. If I spot an issue, more than likely it is a mirror of something within myself that needs work. The late, great Dr. Rev. Johnny Coleman said, "If you spot it, you got it."

The best thing we can do as we make our way through life is to work on ourselves, apply all these wonderful spiritual laws that we're learning, to make progress and evolve spiritually. Life can deal us blow after blow, but all of it can be eased by accepting the lesson and manifesting a better life experience.

"Work hard at your job and you can make a living. Work hard on yourself and you can make a fortune." —Jim Rohn

The year the world stood still has shown us how much a touch, a hug, an embrace actually means. At the time, we could only touch people with sight and sound. I say I love you a lot more now than I ever did before. I don't wait for them to say it. We'll think, oh they know that. We become so familiar we forget how much they mean to us and neglect to tell them so.

Those people in my inner circle? I am more appreciative of them. Acknowledging their life efforts, holding space for them. Being that one voice that will ride for them when they want to accomplish their dreams and goals, and being that support when things don't go quite as planned.

People have done some things to that word love, and it means different things to every person. The people in my life have come to know that that word means I honor you, I respect you, and … I'll always have your back.

My Time in the Sun by Naleighna Kai

Chicago, Illinois
Twelve years later

"The first lady was a prostitute," Terrence Henderson bellowed loud enough to carry the entire length of the church sanctuary and echo from the cathedral ceilings.

All eyes were focused on the richly-dressed minister swaggering past the organ, down the plush maroon carpet of the center aisle, then around the maple wood pews filled with morning worshippers.

"A fourteen-year-old prostitute," he continued. "Not the kind of woman we want our little girls and young women to emulate."

Aridell Henderson Slaughter stood, joined by several other members of the Mothers Board, as she said, "Get thee behind me Satan. And *stay* there."

Sam, the choir director, shouted, "Have you lost your cotton-picking, chicken-plucking mind, mother—" he caught himself before adding the last, more profane part of that Southern saying. "How dare you put her on blast like that."

The silence was nothing short of mind-blowing. Slowly,

murmurs became whispers. Those whispers became a collective voice. That collective voice became a roar of discontent so loud it could have broken the stained-glass window of Christ holding out the goblet of wine to Mary Magdalene.

Kari Baltimore's heart rate sped up to the point where that life-sustaining organ nearly burst from her chest. She brushed a hand down her thighs to smooth the lavender silk dress that draped her curvaceous frame. She glanced at her husband in the pulpit, noticing the second he quickly shuttered his shock as he stood and moved to the edge of the dais.

Pastor Tony Baltimore's hand went up. Voices trickled back down to whispers, then silence slowly descended once again.

"And you're saying this in front of the entire congregation hoping to achieve what, Minister Henderson?" Tony challenged, his sun-kissed complexion aflame with angry color. "To somehow make me ashamed of my wife? To make the members turn against her?"

For a second, the confidence that had been so evident in Terrence's arrogant demeanor slipped. But only for a second. Because the church's board and deacons suddenly rounded him in what seemed to be a show of support.

Kari zeroed in on their solemn expressions which didn't show one ounce of surprise. Evidently, this outburst was a long time in the making.

The fire in Tony's dark brown eyes would normally be enough to quell the most disruptive of people. But not Terrence Henderson. Ever since he'd been ordained to preach by some still-yet-to-be-identified pastor in California where he once lived, the ambitious minister had his sights on being the pastor of the church founded by his great-great grandfather, the good Reverend Jacob Lee Henderson. The position of pastor had been held for four generations of Henderson men. That is, until a scandal with one of the members forced Terrence Henderson's father to make an exit stage left—with teenage mistress in tow—long before the son of his wife had come of age to enter the pulpit.

A board of deacons and trustees had conducted a series of interviews and background checks, searching for a new pastor to lead the modest congregation. Overlooking a slightly flawed past, they'd deemed Anthony "Tony" J. Baltimore worthy to make the cut. If Kari had undergone the same rigorous scrutiny, they might have seen that she had a little baggage *and* a carry-on.

Tony pinned his focus on Terrence, his shoulders tense with conviction as he said, "This woman is not just my wife, she's my partner in helping people in this community find the God they stopped serving a long time ago. She's a spiritual ambassador who helps people find peace when there's so little of it in other aspects of their lives." Admidst a round of Amen's, he moved down the aisle until he was toe-to-toe with Terrence, towering over him by a few inches. "And you couldn't even come at me in a way that was decent and in order, like a board meeting. No, you took the coward's way and tried to shame her publicly in the middle of Sunday morning service."

The members—from the choir, musicians, all the way to the usher board—were on their feet, some voicing their support of Tony, but a surprising number of them siding with Terrence. A good majority of the rest of them stayed silent watching the fireworks as though they couldn't believe something this scandalous would unfold in Sunday service right between prayer and scripture.

"And the first lady hasn't stood up to say it isn't true," Terrence challenged with a haughty lift of his chin.

"That's because her husband's defending her honor and her character," Sister Terry interjected. "And she's doing what a first lady should do—she's letting him."

Several choruses of "Amen" and "that's right, my sister",

"you'd better say that" rang through the sanctuary.

The one thing Kari feared most was playing out right before her eyes, hurting the man she loved in a way she never wanted. At that moment, she wished she could vanish into thin air as Enoch had when he went to be with the Lord. No natural death there. One minute he was, and then he wasn't.

The hard part about all this? Her husband didn't know anything about this fragment of her past. She had buried it so deep, even she couldn't remember the details. That was supposed to be a good thing. Fresh start. New life.

How sad that one man's ambition could serve as another woman's destruction.

Get your copy of *My Time in the Sun* wherever books are sold.

Loving Me for Me by Naleighna Kai

Fourteen-year-old Reign was forced to get up in front of the church and apologize for shaming her mother by getting pregnant. She complied but was angry the entire time. Especially since she was fully aware of things going on behind the scenes. While she still held the microphone, she paused and then ended her apology with, "But I have a question, though. Is it only the girls you want to apologize just because you can see what we've done?" She rubbed her hand over her extended belly as the question drew murmurs of discontent. "Dawn got pregnant. No one asked Mason to come up here and apologize. Alexa got knocked up. No one made Eric say he was sorry. My brothers weren't made to get up here either."

The congregation roared with disapproval aimed directly at her. Some of them stood, raising their voices in contempt.

"Now, I know it does not excuse what I did," Reign continued, holding up a hand to signal they should quiet down because she wasn't done. "But I'm just saying Brother Harold's been sleeping with Sister Odessa's husband for the past two years. Everybody knows it." She focused on the golden man whose face turned a magnificent red. "Oh, and I don't see Sister Justine and Brother Martin up here apologizing for getting busy in the choir room during rehearsal when the pastor's wife caught 'em a few months ago."

"Now, wait a minute," Brother Martin stood, shaking his fist at Reign. His wife yanked him back down in the pew, then slapped her purse on top of his head nearly knocking him unconscious. Sister Justine left her husband's side and tried to run from the church. Her exit was blocked by the ushers who seemed to be having a grand old time with all of the skeletons creaking out of the closet and running up the church aisle as if the devil was on their heels. One of them, Sister Dorothy, even managed to give Reign the thumbs up sign, so she'd keep the party going.

"I'm just saying let's keep it fair," she said, ducking out of the reach of Deacon Jones who was making an attempt to snatch the microphone from her. "A sin's a sin. I think everybody should take a turn up here." She gestured toward Deacon Byrne as she slid up the aisle, managing to still be heard over all the chaos. "That is a *whole bottle* of Dr. Tichenor's in your pocket 'cause you need a little nip of that eighty-proof every now. Nobody needs fresh breath that bad." She winked at him, and even his wife laughed. "My mama told me that one."

The entire congregation was now on their feet, in heated conversations, some arguing about the truth she let spill. Choir members hastily left their seats. A few of them managed to tip out of the back door to the lower level before she let loose on them, too. The usher board had closed the rear doors so no one could run out that way. One of them sprinted down the right side aisle to get to the choir entrance to block that as well.

Reign slid a sly look to her fuming mother, who was dressed in the pristine white uniform of the pastor's personal nurse and was sitting in a special seat near the pulpit. "And the only reason my mother's on the nurse's board," Reign said, keeping a steely glare on her mother. "Taking care of the pastor, getting his water and handkerchiefs, fixing all that good food and baking those sweet potato pies especially for him, is 'cause she's hoping for a little … *sin* of her own."

"I knew it," the First Lady said, waggling a finger at Thelma, wide brim hat tipping almost off her head. She nearly climbed over the pew, aiming to get to Reign's mother. Two women nearest her, held the stout woman back.

Reign looked toward the red-faced Pastor who was fit to be tied. "And doesn't look like he's turning down nothing but his collar, so maybe I should pass the mic to him. Come to think of it, Brother Jimmy, Brother Patrick, and Brother Russell need some time up here, too." She moved up the middle aisle and back toward the pulpit ignoring the three men in question. "Each one of them offered me some money—for the baby's sake. That's what they said. But they wanted a *little something* in return. They seemed really happy that I was pregnant 'cause that meant I couldn't get knocked up again." She swept a gaze across the congregation as Sister Delores yanked the microphone from her hand. Reign dashed toward the choir stand to snatch another one from where the organist played. "And they're not the only ones up in here who did that. I've got nine offers from church men alone and close to $9,536.50." She waggled an index finger. "And don't forget the fifty cents. That's a lot of dough, especially for a sinner like me." She shrugged as if she hadn't set the church on holy fire. "So let's be fair about this sin thing."

"That's enough, young lady," the pastor said from the pulpit, gesturing for someone to grab her. Reign faked left, then moved until she was in the far left aisle blocked in by a few folks who were grinning at her efforts and didn't let the deacons near her.

"Oh, so I'm a *young lady* now?" Reign shot back, glowering angrily at him. "When you told my mother that she needed to bring her *little whore* before the church to apologize."

"No he didn't," Sister Mabel shouted.

"But you didn't make your nieces get up here when *they* got pregnant. Or any of the boys right here in this church who made them that way. I count about twelve so far. And that's not including the ones who had abortions." Reign snapped her fingers as realization hit. "But wait a minute, that counts as sin, too, right? But it's not one that you can see."

Gasps echoed throughout the congregation.

"So which is it? Whore or young lady?" she taunted, stretching out her hands as if in supplication. "Either way, I'm just saying—a sin is a sin. Let the church say 'Amen'."

Get your copy of *Loving Me for Me* wherever books are sold.

King of Devon by Naleighna Kai

"What do you mean she's in labor? Jai gripped the edge of the desk, with the phone pressed to his ear. "That's ... well, that's impossible."

His heart slammed in his chest when Kelly Peterson didn't retract her statement.

Everything was happening much faster than he expected. A patient, who fell into a coma after a tragic car accident, had been in his health center for a year. Her circumstances took a downward and unfortunate turn because she had not been pregnant when she arrived. He, along with all of his male employees, were now under intense investigation. Didn't help matters any that almost all of the employees were ex-felons who were aiming for a second chance in life. Even worse, his holistic practices at Chetan had drawn the ire of the medical industry because of the substantial success rate. The Health Bureau had been trying to find any reason to shut him down. Temple Devaughn's newborn baby would provide a direct avenue for that to happen.

The media was abuzz over the situation and their actions were being fueled by Donald Amos, a former high-level member of The Castle who was itching to regain his seat on the board. Not going to happen with Jai and his eight fellow

Kings at the helm. Dr. Taylor had said Temple would carry to term. Seven, almost eight months in and evidently, nature had other plans. His life was about to hit the porcelain goddess and circle the bowl for a few rounds before the royal flush. "In labor, right now?"

"Yes," Kelly whispered. "Right now."

He rounded the glass desk and grabbed a leather briefcase, then jammed the meeting notes he'd been scanning inside. "Are the paramedics on their way?"

"They're about twenty minutes out," she replied, and he steeled himself for even more bad news. "Dr. Taylor is in Africa on a health mission, and isn't expected back until next week. So, no one from her team is at the hospital right now. That means whoever is going to be part of the delivery hasn't been briefed on the delicacy of this particular situation. Overall, things are about to be pretty damn interesting."

And that would present a problem within itself. Jai had chosen Dr. Julie Taylor because she was not afraid of the challenges Temple's pregnancy presented. Every other doctor had taken a hard pass. Their careers were on the line, and the potential failure could damage their reputations and their licenses. Julie had been a family practitioner who changed her discipline once she realized how few OB/GYNs were in Africa, and how desperately they were needed.

"I'm on my way," he said to Kelly as he made it to the front door of his home. "Thanks for all you do."

"It's always a pleasure, Jai."

Twelve minutes later, he arrived at the glass-and-steel building that housed the Chetan Healing Center and parked in his reserved spot near the entrance. This frantic pace wasn't a good way to start the morning, but the situation called for him to be on high alert.

The moment the smoke-tinted doors slid open and he set foot across the threshold—all while balancing his phone, tablet, and briefcase—Kelly rushed toward him. Her ivory skin was flushed to crimson and her reddish-brown hair plastered to the side of her face as though she'd sprinted an entire marathon. Not a good sign.

"We can't reach Temple's mother or fiancé," she said, gasping for breath. "The center has power of attorney for health care. You'll have to act on our patient's behalf."

A chill passed through Jai, rendering him almost numb. He handed off his briefcase and accepted the documents she held as he tried to come to terms with what her words meant. "Power of attorney for an issue that happened at Chetan, yes. This is something entirely different."

"No, it isn't," she countered, hooking her arm under his and directing him to where the paramedics were wheeling a gurney across the threshold toward the waiting ambulance. "Go with her to the hospital."

"Hey, be gentle," he warned the crew navigating the concrete. "She's not a piece of meat."

The men didn't stop or bat an eye. "She's comatose," the slimmer one of the pair said. "She can't feel it anyway."

"That is *not* acceptable," Jai roared, and Kelly held his arm in a vice-like grip to keep him in place. "What if she was your mother . . . or sister? Treat. Her. Gently."

Kelly relaxed her hold on him, and Jai threw her a glance, expressing his thanks without speaking. She nodded in response and gave him a slight smile.

The men halted a few feet from the vehicle, shared a speaking glance that revealed their irritation, but they complied by significantly slowing their movements.

Jai stepped into the back of the ambulance and perched on a silver bench, watching as they situated the IV, then strapped the patient in before the burly one ran to the front and sped away from the sidewalk.

The fifteen-minute drive was tense and silent, except for the blare of the siren and the furtive glances the two-member crew sent his way—one from the rearview mirror. The ambulance pulled into the emergency bay of Meridian Hospital. A team of nurses and a salt-and-pepper haired doctor with a dour expression swept out of the doors and scurried toward the vehicle.

He extended a hand to Jai. "I'm Dr. Christian."

When the two nurses gripped the silver railings, the shorter of the paramedics said, "Treat her like glass or this guy will have a conniption."

His partner nodded in Jai's direction and scowled.

"That was uncalled for," Dr. Christian said, his tone sharp and forbidding, matching the frown that appeared on his face.

"We don't have the time to belabor the point that comatose doesn't mean deceased," Jai shot back, glaring at the two men who were ignoring the warning looks from the nurses.

Dr. Christian flinched, then his head whipped around to Jai. "Wait a minute. Did you say comatose?"

Jai kept his gaze on the men and didn't bother to answer the question.

The doctor recovered his composure and gave the two emergency personnel a stern look as he warned, "You'll hear about this later."

"Whatever, man." The stockier one waved him off.

Jai made a mental note to address the entire situation when things calmed down. No telling what other process those two had let slide. While he understood that most of their fellow paramedics had been on strike for a while, their attitude was out of order.

The preparation for the baby's arrival soon became a synchronicity of nurses pulling together all needed materials, equipment, and getting Jai in place. The fact that the doctor had been thrown for a loop became evident in the furrowed brow, anxious expression, and solemn bearing.

"You're the father?" Dr. Christian asked, suiting up and gesturing for Nurse Jennifer to outfit Jai in the same manner.

"No, I have power of attorney to see to Temple's well-being."

Dr. Christian lowered his mask to ask, "So, she was pregnant when she arrived at your center?"

"The notes are all here, doctor," Jai said, passing him a set of documents Kelly had the presence of mind to compile and place in a manila folder.

The doctor slipped off his gloves, scanned the pages, then blinked several times before focusing on Jai. "She's *that* woman? From the news?"

"Yes," Jai answered through his teeth and offered nothing more since the rest of the nursing staff had turned curious gazes in their direction.

Dr. Christian held up a hand to keep Jai from moving forward. "So, we're going to do a C-section to get this over and done with."

"Dr. Taylor already had a plan in place to induce a semi-natural labor," Jai said, flipping the page and putting an index finger on the summary paragraph of the health plan he'd worked out with Dr. Taylor. Her method would be best for Temple's overall health."

"That might be true," he countered, switching out his gloves. "But I'm not Dr. Taylor and what I say in this hospital goes."

"I get that," Jai shot back, moving until only a few feet stood between them. "And I'm still saying, do not cut her unless it's absolutely necessary. You haven't even assessed her to see what the best course should be."

Jai had researched several cases that were similar to Temple's in that the women were also pregnant and in a coma. The difference had been in the fact that in the information he came across, the women were already pregnant before going into the coma. Temple's pregnancy occurred several months *after* she arrived at Chetan. The plan Dr. Taylor put in place meant a possible chance for Temple to fully recover after the birth and resume treatment at Chetan. She'd need special care, and he along with his staff, were well prepared for that contingency.

The nurses were now tending to Temple, but moving at such a slow pace Jai was certain they were listening intently to the exchange.

"Dr. Taylor is willing to take chances that I am not," he admitted. "It's my license and practice that would be at stake, not hers. The patient isn't having a normal delivery process and that bears a great deal of consideration. It's possible she would not survive. Be more merciful that way."

"And your attitude is the very thing I'd hoped to avoid. She's been through enough," Jai said, giving the people gathered around them a cursory glance. "Having to go through a C-Section would be unnecessarily traumatic."

"No more traumatic than what happened to put her in this condition," Dr. Christian shot back, gesturing to Temple's belly. "And it happened in your special little facility. I don't even know why you're here. Aren't you under investigation as one of the men who might have impregnated her?"

Jaidev Maharaj saw red.

Get your copy of *King of Devon* wherever books are sold.

King of Durabia by Naleighna Kai

No good deed goes unpunished, or that's how Ellena Kiley feels after she rescues a child and the former Crown Prince of Durabia offers to marry her.

Kamran learns of a nefarious plot to undermine his position with the Sheikh and jeopardize his ascent to the throne. He's unsure how Ellena, the fiery American seductress, fits into the plan but she's a secret weapon he's unwilling to relinquish.

Ellena is considered a sister by the Kings of the Castle and her connection to Kamran challenges her ideals, her freedoms, and her heart. Plus, loving him makes her a potential target for his enemies. When Ellena is kidnapped, Kamran is forced to bring in the Kings.

In the race against time to rescue his woman and defeat his enemies, the kingdom of Durabia will never be the same.

Chapter 1

"You risked your life for my grandson," Sheikh Aayan said, his voice echoing through the ornate throne room. "Ask for anything and I will see what can be done."

Ellena scanned the expectant faces of the throngs of people who had gathered for this unexpected audience with the ruler of Durabia. Most of their tunics and dishdashas differed from her casual attire of a simple white blouse and black slacks. "Thank you, but that isn't necessary. I did what anyone would do."

"Evidently, not everyone," he said, and his angry glare focused on the bodyguard, caregivers, and everyone who had stood by when Javed, the little royal, had swept past Ellena and landed on the moving conveyor belt.

All of them had frozen in place the moment Javed brushed against the rubber bounding strip and was sucked into the void. The video of Ellena dropping her tote bag, diving in after him, and cradling him in her arms as they were both tossed through the maze of steel and vinyl, all while being battered by suitcases and duffel bags alike, went viral.

Ellena had closed her eyes, bracing under each blow. Javed's laughter was a stark contrast to her pain. The cameras caught everything, including the tail end of the journey when Ellena tumbled out of the final drop onto another belt and finally into the metal cart that would carry the luggage onto the plane. Security finally found their legs and scrambled to make it to Ellena and the little boy before they sustained further injuries. Well, before she did. Her fleshy body was all the protection that Javed needed.

Javed Khan, a great grandson of the royal family, was completely unharmed. Ellena, on the day of arrival for a class reunion vacation, had to be rushed to the hospital. They kept her overnight. She sustained a few cuts and bruises that matched the dent in her ego when the entire world saw her tossed head over ass multiple times. And when the adrenaline wore off and the fear kicked in, the little royal refused to let her go. He even had to travel in the emergency transport with her because none of the guards or caregivers managed to force him to release his hold on Ellena.

Now she stood in a palace situated in the heart of a metropolis in the Middle East with a décor that was unrivaled by anything she'd ever seen. Gold—everything was layered with it—the walls, doors, accented by purples and reds that added a sultry warmth to all of the opulence of the furniture, paintings, and draperies covering massive windows.

"Well, to be honest, I haven't wanted much," she said with a nervous laugh. "And the only thing I don't have is a husband. But I'd love to have a place here in Durabia, where I can come and go as I please. If that is at all possible."

"Done," the Sheikh said, beckoning to the man who had visited the hospital twice to see about her condition. "Kamran, come."

"Wait. What?" She laughed and rested a hand on her ample bosom. "An apartment, really?"

"Your new husband," he answered with a grand gesture that would have made Vanna White proud. "This is my oldest son."

The man was drop-dead gorgeous. Olive complexion, dark hair, goatee neatly trimmed to perfection, and piercing brown eyes that missed nothing. He was more suited to a fashion runway than a palace. Truthfully, she wasn't sure if it was the tunics, neat beards, head coverings or what. Durabia seemed to have no shortage of handsome men. But the Sheikh's son was a masterpiece, exuding the kind of confidence that came with a man who was certain of his place in the world. His gaze swept across her face with a complexion slightly darker than his olive tone, then quickly covered the distance over her curves, then his lips lifted in a warm, appreciative smile that practically lit up his dark brown eyes and sent heat straight to places that had been dormant since the Queen of Sheba caused King Solomon to lose his entire mind.

Ellena shook her head, clearing her mind of all manner of wickedness that came after that wonderful assessment. "I think you misunderstood. I was joking about the husband part. The apartment, time share or whatever you call them here, that's all I really want."

"You will have both," the Sheikh commanded with a nod of finality no one would dare to question. "A husband and a place here. My son needs a wife and you mentioned you do not have a husband. Problem solved."

"But doesn't he have to give you heirs or something?" She instinctively brought her hands near her belly. "My eggs are old enough to be married and have children of their own by now."

First, a roar of laughter went up from him. A few moments later, it was mirrored by everyone standing around her. Yes, that line was funny, but the one thing she understood was the unfairness of the situation. At least for Kamran. And that was no laughing matter.

The Sheikh waved away that thought. "That will not be a concern. He is unable to give you or any woman children. And a woman of African descent will never sit on the Durabian throne. We are safe on that score."

A shadow of sadness flickered in Kamran's eyes and his skin flushed a shade darker. Ellena tried to read a deeper meaning into his father's words. She still came up with *unfair*. "So, you just throw him to a random woman because he can't give you an heir? He is *still* a man. He *still* has value," she insisted. "A brain, intelligence, and a purpose." She inhaled, trying to tamp down on her anger. "The apartment is fine, Sheikh. Thank you, but I will not be foisted on a man who has no say in the matter. That's downright cruel."

A gasp came from the core of people around them before silence descended in the room. Even Kamran flinched.

The Sheikh's face darkened with anger as he slowly came to his feet. "Are you refusing—"

"Give me nine days—"

All eyes focused on the handsome man, who left his father's side and moseyed toward her like some type of Arabian cowboy. All swagger, no gun necessary.

"Give me nine days," he repeated and moved across the expensive Persian carpet until he stood in front of her, towering over her near six-foot height by three inches of his own. "Nine days for me to show you Durabia, to answer any questions you may have. To let you explore the place, the people, the culture. Then you decide."

Ellena found it hard to catch her breath. The man was so virile she felt warm all the way to her follicles. "Nine days? I have to go home. I have a job back there. I used all of my vacation and two of my sick days for this trip."

"Your job?" he asked, frowning as though he couldn't fathom what the word meant.

"Yes. A job. Nine to five. Benefits. All of that. You know, what regular folks do to keep an address."

Kamran remained silent for a few moments as he peered at her. "How much do they pay you?"

She winced, then flickered a gaze to his right and felt the intensity of everyone's attention. "It doesn't matter."

"How much?" He beckoned for her to come nearer. "Whisper it to me."

Ellena hesitated a moment, then complied, moving so close she inhaled the intoxicating scent of sandalwood. She managed to whisper an answer, then inched back to put a little distance between them.

"For the rest of your life?" he asked, his tone and wide eyes reflecting the incredulity registered in his facial expression.

"Until I'm sixty-seven and retire," she replied, daunted by his tone. "But there's also health benefits and other factors that I can't put a number on."

Kamran blinked as though doing a set of mental calculations and coming up with what probably amounted to simple interest on his bank account. "Give me the particulars and I will wire the money into your account."

She parted her lips to protest but he held up a hand. "Saying yes to taking me as your husband is still your choice. With this, I am simply ensuring your peace of mind. And as a gift for your kindness, your selflessness in saving a child who was a stranger to you."

let out a long, slow breath, because staying here ... nently, marrying him, would be a lost cause. She loved job as a personal assistant at Vantage Point. Alejandro ...eyes, a "Fixer" of everything from political and corporate espionage, to terrorist attacks, was the absolute best person to work for. And she loved the predictability of her life. Traveling overseas was the most adventurous event in her life. Still, curiosity won out over common sense and she said, "All right. Thank you."

"Now we go about the business of getting to know one another," he said, smiling as though her consent brought him much pleasure. Evidently, he wanted this to happen and the intensity of his gaze bore into her soul. "So that you can make an informed decision, yes?"

She glanced over his shoulder, taking in some of the envious looks a few of the women tried to hide. "Why are you doing this?" she asked him. "Why are you allowing them to serve you up to some foreign woman as if you do not have value?"

"Because I recognize this is God's will," he answered. "And who am I to leave a precious gift unwrapped?"

Her eyebrows drew in, as she tried to decipher the hidden meaning behind his words. The man had a peaceful, confident air but also a playful vibe about him.

"Yes, that was a double entendre." His smile widened and she could swear the heavens opened up and smiled with him.

Good Lord, I'm in trouble.

Get your copy of *King of Durabia* wherever books are sold.

About the Author

Naleighna Kai is the *USA TODAY*, *Essence®* national bestselling and award-winning author of several women's fiction, contemporary fiction, Christian fiction, Romance, erotica, and science fiction novels that plumb the depth of unique relationships and women's issues. She is also a contributor to a *New York Times* bestseller, one of AALBC's 100 Top Authors, a member of CVS Hall of Fame, Mercedes Benz Mentor Award Nominee, and the E. Lynn Harris Author of Distinction.

In addition to successfully cracking the code of landing a deal for herself and others with a major publishing house, she continues to "pay it forward" by organizing the annual Cavalcade of Authors and NK's Tribe Called Success which gives readers intimate access to the most accomplished writing talent today. She also serves as CEO of The Macro Group, LLC which offers aspiring and established authors assistance with ghostwriting, developmental editing, publishing, marketing, and other services to jump-start or enhance their writing careers.

www.naleighnakai.com

FB: @naleighnakai
IG: @naleighnakai
TW: @naleighnakai

The Merry Hearts Inspirational Series will warm your heart
and touch your soul . . .